THE KITCHEN CABINET

THE KITCHEN CABINET

A year of recipes, flavours, facts & stories for food lovers

ANNIE GRAY

Foreword by JAY RAYNER

Contents

Foreword

Like many of the very best British ideas, *The Kitchen Cabinet* was born in a room above a pub: a dimly lit one near London's Old Street roundabout, with modishly bare floorboards, trestle tables and the most functional of chairs. The non-broadcast pilots recorded there late in 2011 were a bare-bones affair. There was a tiny audience, mostly made up of staff from the production company who had been asked nicely if they wouldn't mind staying a little late that evening. There was a handful of food-based questions for them to read out, and two sets of potential panellists for them to put those questions to. Once the first lot of candidates had been put through their paces they were shifted out, and the next lot brought in.

I have been involved with many radio and TV show launches over the years. They always change markedly between the pilot and the programme that makes it to air. Not *The Kitchen Cabinet*. It was completely itself right from the very off: a seemingly loose-limbed, enthusiastic burst of bubbling food chat of the sort you might hope to find at the greediest of dinner tables.

In the early days of 2012, as the first trial series of four episodes became a second series of six, I would often hear people describe it as 'a kind of food version of *Gardeners' Question Time*'. They didn't know quite how right they were. The production company Somethin' Else had not long before won the prized contract to produce the venerable BBC Radio 4 gardening show, which had been on the air since 1947. Having executed that successfully, without enraging the notoriously loyal Radio 4 audience, they had started thinking. Were there other subjects to which the format, such as it is – a panel of experts, asked questions by an audience – might be applied? Food was the obvious answer.

I was originally approached to try out as a panellist. I declined. It was obvious to me that the people who got that gig would need many qualities, chief among them being the ability to rattle off the outline of a recipe to order. After more than 20 years as the restaurant critic for the *Observer*, I do know my food. I'm great at eating it, and not bad at writing about it. But the recipe thing wasn't a part of my skill set. I grandly suggested they let me have a go at chairing this new show instead. I'm grateful they gave me a shot.

Because I was spot on. Even during those try-outs above the pub, it became obvious that being a *Kitchen Cabinet* panellist would be a tricky job; one that the panellists would have to make look easy. Of course, they do need to be able to do the instant recipe thing. A particular food specialism is important too; we want a show that represents and reflects the myriad cultures that make up the UK, through those communities' cooking traditions. But they also need to have a hinterland, a world beyond the table, which enables them to place those dishes in some sort of context. They need a grand store of anecdotes and opinions, strongly held, however ludicrous. *The Kitchen Cabinet* is nothing if it's not entertaining.

The panellists need to be extroverts who are ready to grab their moment, but also team players who know when to shut up. They need to be the kind of people you want at your table. Early on, we concluded that this was not really a job for the legions of celebrity chefs who were already hogging the airwaves. They obviously know their stuff, but that doesn't necessarily mean they would be great at communicating it. We are certainly not against a bit of formal training. A number of our panellists are classically trained chefs. More importantly for us, however, is the fact that those trained chefs also happen to be hilarious. We have food writers, well-travelled wits and raconteurs, cookery competition winners, and academics covering a variety of food and cooking disciplines. I may be biased, but I think we really have assembled the dream dinner-party guestlist. On page xv you'll find a full cast list of *The Kitchen Cabinet* regulars whose wisdom, and belly-obsessed take on the world, has contributed to this book.

As we started our journeys around Britain, crisscrossing the entire UK, from its southernmost tip to its northernmost cities, from Belfast to Cardiff to Edinburgh and back again, one thing became clear. Having a knowledgeable panel was great. It was essential. But our live audience is what really makes *The Kitchen Cabinet*. On page 74 you'll find one of this book's 'Tea Breaks'. It describes how each episode is put together. We want the show to sound freewheeling and effortless. Achieving that takes serious effort. We spend a lot of time choosing our subjects for each week, depending on the season and where we're going to be, discussing them with our panellists and guests, and coming up with the outline of a script.

But it's the audience questions, selected in the hour before we start recording, that are the show's beating heart. I'd be lying if I pretended we didn't go hunting for certain questions to fit the direction that the themes we've prepared are going. But if a belter of a question comes in, we'll throw stuff out just to make room for it. And even if we don't broadcast them all, we always have space in the script for four general questions, which could be about anything at all, and usually are.

Even in the spring of 2020, when the pandemic forced us to halt recording the show in front of live audiences, those questions remained front and centre. We solicited them from social media and via email. Later, when the BBC created a piece of tech allowing for a virtual audience, we were able to record the show in front of some of the largest crowds we'd ever had and take their questions in person, even if some of those people were probably sitting on their sofas in their underwear. After all, we have never had a dress code.

From the start, we knew what *The Kitchen Cabinet* was not about: dietary advice, nutrition, food poverty, economics, politics and ethics. Not because those subjects aren't important. They're absolutely crucial, but they are also covered by other programmes on the BBC. We are here to chat, not lecture. That said, our broad historical and cultural approach to the joys of eating means we often do get into this stuff, but in a historical context.

There is, for example, a variety of stews made across the UK, each with different names: the likes of Liverpool's lobscouse, the Lancashire hotpot and both Monmouth stew and cawl from Wales. I now know better than to claim they all have exactly the same recipe. As we've learnt on our travels, the way to make regional dishes can vary even from household to household. But at base, they came about in the same way: from the need to stretch a small amount of, perhaps, the less prime cuts to feed the maximum number of people. We are fascinated by origin stories like this: of pies and pasties, of smoked foods and long-stewed vegetable dishes. We are intrigued by the way the earliest of mass food producers influenced what's on our shelves today, and how class divides have defined the way we eat now. We are here for it all.

And we're here to taste it all. Possibly the bravest thing we did was put eating noises on BBC Radio 4. At the live recordings, the panellists' table has always ended up being laid with a ludicrous and wantonly random buffet of dishes, some specific to the place we have been visiting, others made by the panellists themselves. The tasting of those foods quickly became a feature of the show. Partly, I think that was because it required me to ask the team to talk with their mouths full or while dribbling profusely. Somehow, we seem to have been forgiven for our terribly bad manners.

The big question is how could we represent this seemingly freewheeling, multi-faceted food chat in a book? The honest answer is, how could we not? There have been well over 200 episodes of *The Kitchen Cabinet*. That's a huge number of questions answered, and an awful lot of food stories told. We have visited cities, towns and villages all over the country, and met literally thousands of like-minded people. That has created a massive and detailed brains trust of hungry knowledge, anecdote, ephemera and ideas for the table. Mixed in with quite a lot of spiky opinion.

We have arranged all of that by month because, even in a world of mass production and supermarkets, the seasons still do have huge sway over what and how we eat. This really is *The Kitchen Cabinet* year. We've even collected the key dates in the calendar because we've always been there for the eating opportunities presented by a festival, be it Burns Night, the Hindu celebration of Holi or Hallowe'en. You'll find the key flavours and crops associated with each month, along with a veneration of a particular cheese. We do love a good cheese.

And each month you'll find us in a different UK town or city. That presents the opportunity to talk about those specific regional dishes and food traditions and the local food heroes responsible for them. There are also the talking points that have made our greedy minds whir: our favourite food-related films, for example; the sounds we love in the kitchen or the engineering of a crisp sandwich. (Soft white bread is vital, as you ask). As with *The Kitchen Cabinet* itself, we are not about definitive opinions. One of the things we've learnt over the years is that we can all wildly disagree with each other, sometimes on the smallest of details, and yet find those disagreements hugely informative. Sometimes we even change our minds.

And, of course, you'll find lots and lots of terrific ideas for lovely things to eat. Not all of them involve cheese, bacon or a swim in the deep-fat fryer. Many of them are meat free, dairy free or vegan. What you won't find is much in the way of precise recipes. At the risk of sounding like some faux shaman, this has always been *The Kitchen Cabinet* way. All of us on the show have at some point published formal recipes. We know just how much testing and refining it takes to get them right. Our panellists only get about 10 minutes notice of the questions they'll be asked at each recording. As a result, the suggestions they come up with – for ways to make a staple ingredient interesting again, the uses for something obscure, or perhaps for a dish that will get a refusenik engaged again – are necessarily broad brushstroke. It's the same with this book.

The reality is that outside of disciplines like pastry and baking, where measurements are vital, the vast majority of the best things to eat start as a set of ideas, or perhaps simply a question. What would happen if I put this with that? Could those vegetables be roasted with that herb? Will I be judged if I slap that ingredient between two pieces of white bread and shove it in a toastie maker just to see what happens? The answer to the last question is never, or at least not by us. *The Kitchen Cabinet* has always been a place for people who live to eat and so is this book. Just as with the shows that we broadcast through the year, we want you to feel it's a friend. We hope you find it thoroughly nourishing, in all ways.

Jay Rayner

Who's who on *The Kitchen Cabinet*

Since *The Kitchen Cabinet* sallied forth for its first-ever airing in 2012, we've had a changing line-up of panellists. Some you'll recognise as long-standing voices, others have come and gone. But everyone has helped make it into the show it is today. For anyone who hasn't listened to every single episode, made copious notes, and then rushed out to buy all our books and watch our other shows, talks and tomfoolery, the main people you'll encounter within these pages are:

Tim Anderson: From Wisconsin by way of Japan, author of five books on Japanese cookery, restaurateur, *Masterchef* winner and a beer expert to boot.

Prof. Peter Barham: Emeritus Professor of Physics at the University of Bristol, and our chief molecular gastronomist. Spends a lot of time with penguins.

Jordan Bourke: Irish chef, food writer and expert on Korean cookery. Believes nothing isn't improved by a teaspoon of gochujang.

Dr Annie Gray: East Anglia-based, our resident food historian and the reason we have a mythbuster klaxon. Cheesehead.

Angela Hartnett: Michelin-starred proprietor of restaurants and goddess of sophisticated, yet simple, Italian food.

Tim Hayward: Writer, broadcaster, restaurateur and geek. He likes his bacon inside a hot cross bun.

Anna Jones: Cook, writer and voice of modern vegetarian cooking. The things she can do with feta and a BBQ are inspired (as you shall find out).

Nisha Katona MBE: Liverpool-based barrister-cum-restaurateur and author, she's the curry evangelist and entrepreneur who runs the Indian restaurant chain Mowgli.

Asma Khan: Indian-born British chef, author and owner of the Darjeeling Express in Covent Garden, she's our newest panellist who won us over with lashings of ghee.

Dr Zoe Laughlin: Our resident materials expert – a designer, maker and materials engineer obsessed with the art and science of stuff. Her greatest pleasure is eating in the bath.

Sue Lawrence: What Sue doesn't know about the regional recipes of Scotland ain't worth knowing. Born in Dundee, raised in Edinburgh, she's a cook and food writer who's lived in France, Finland, Australia and Germany.

Lizzie Mabbott: The Anglo-Chinese self-taught cook and food writer who's always hungry. Known for her food blog *Hollow Legs* and cookbooks on Chinese cuisine.

Rachel McCormack: Glaswegian whisky writer, Catalan food expert and raconteur du jour. Can drink everyone else under the table.

Paula McIntyre MBE: The doyenne of Northern Irish cookery, a chef, food broadcaster, writer and teacher who ensures she's never far from a Tayto sarnie.

Andi Oliver: Hackney-based, voice of a jazzy angel, crosses with ease between Caribbean, Scandinavian and British food traditions. Hates Spam.

Rob Owen-Brown: Classically trained chef, restaurateur, caterer and sometimes boat dweller. Once disappeared for 3 days after a show as he went fishing with the local butcher.

Jeremy Pang: From a lineage of passionate Chinese cooks, author and founder of the School of Wok and *Ready Steady Cook* star. Keep an eye on what he does with sausages and sugar.

Shelina Permalloo: Expert on Mauritian food, author and 2012 winner of *Masterchef*. Sometimes we pit Shelina and Tim A. against each other for fun.

James 'Jocky' Petrie: Scottish chef, once Head of Development at The Fat Duck, now Group Executive Development Chef for Gordon Ramsay ... need we say more?!

Niki Segnit: Food writer and cook obsessed with flavour, epitomised by her book *The Flavour Thesaurus* and her penchant for trying everything.

Prof. Barry Smith: Our most sensual of panellists, Professor of Philosophy obsessed with the science of eating. And also wine, especially wine.

Prof. Charles Spence: Professor of Experimental Psychology at the University of Oxford and a Director of Kitchen Theory. He and Barry are regular co-conspirators.

Itamar Srulovich: Born in Jerusalem, Itamar's one half of the Middle Eastern food authority Honey and Co. Heed all he says, especially on baking and cooking with fire.

Sumayya Usmani: Born in Karachi, Pakistan, Sumayya is a self-taught cook, food educator and author who lives in Glasgow. She does amazing things with leftover keema.

Sophie Wright: Brought up in the traditions of London's East End, Sophie's our classically trained queen of basically *everything*. She has her own catering company and is a food writer too.

How to use this book

This is your book now. We hope you enjoy it. Like all good food books, we also hope you take it places – your kitchen, your loo, your bedroom – wherever you want to read it. We also hope you don't just read it, but actively use it. You'll find lots of space to add your own notes.

We've also added some handy icons to help you navigate the wonders within:

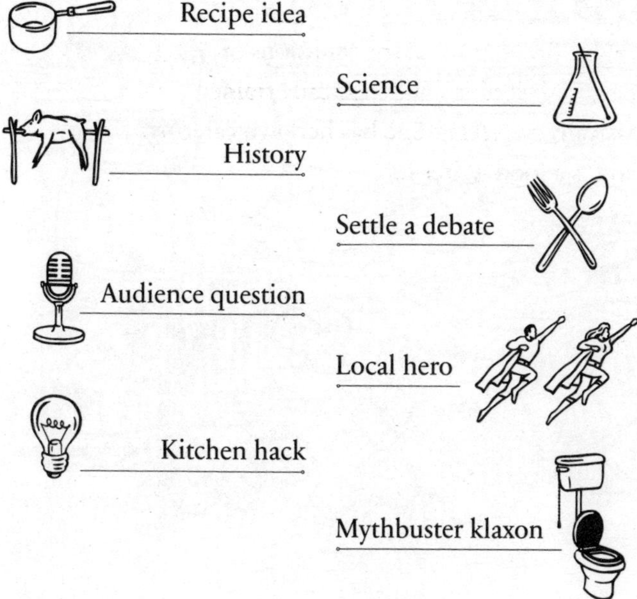

You'll see that some of the key dates have been left blank. We went to print in mid-2021, and between the upheavals of COVID-19 and the simple fact that some things weren't due to happen until the end of 2022, we couldn't confirm all of the dates. Feel free to add them, as well as adding any other things you think are important.

January

Key dates for food fanatics this month:

Twelfth Night (time for twelfth cake, king cake and galette des rois)

Orthodox Christmas (big in Russia, where the Nativity fast ends with sochivo – a Christmas porridge – and moves onto goose, cakes and celebration)

Plough Monday (there's a pudding link, though no definitive recipe)

Burns Night (break out the haggis, whisky and bagpipes)

End of 'Dry' January (we don't judge)

The moon this month is made of **Sage Derby**

Modern Sage Derby is a mottled green block with a mild herb flavour. The original cheese was stripy and punchier. Curds were layered with sage leaves, sometimes pimped with a bit of green from spinach. They were pressed, moulded and aged for a few months, and were in season from autumn to New Year – so now would have been the last chance to enjoy one for another six months. In 2020, **Alan Salt** of the Hartington Creamery put together the first pressed Sage Derby to be made in Derbyshire for about 60 years, just for the TKC panel to devour.

This month *The Kitchen Cabinet* is in **Bakewell** in Derbyshire, known for its tart and pudding, and as the starting point for many an appetite-inducing hike in the Peak District National Park.

Key flavours this month include **citrus**, **kale** and **Jerusalem artichoke**, plus **oysters** and **venison**.

And we are also thinking about:

- Food resolutions
- The best way to peel fresh ginger

- How to make cut herbs last longer
- Our favourite food-related films
- And whether cheese is best eaten before or after dessert

Welcome to Bakewell, gateway to the Peak District, where many a hungry walker has slung their backpack and gone in search of something satisfying to perk them up after a lengthy ramble.

The surrounding countryside is dramatic and inviting, all crags and cliffs, plus the winding River Wye. Bakewell's streets are lined with mellow stone buildings, some of which date from its attempts to compete with nearby Buxton as a spa town and centre for less energetic, genteel saunterings. Austen aficionados will know it as *Pride and Prejudice*'s Lambton, and some of our panel were hoping for Colin Firth in a wet shirt as a special guest (it didn't happen).

Panellist pick: ***New Year resolutions***

Every couple of years we check in with our panellists to see what their culinary New Year resolutions are. These are just a few of their publicly avowed declarations:

Sophie Wright: I've got to stop leaving fatty cast-iron pans in the sink to soak. The next morning, I'm just greeted by horror. My husband is all 'that's a soaker,' but no, I'm going to scrub them. That night.

Andi Oliver: I don't know if it's going to make me a better person, but my mother-in-law has got the most amazing recipe for oxtail and butter beans. She won't let me in the kitchen when she is making it, but I'm determined to get it out of her.

Jordan Bourke: Sorting the drawer of plastic containers. It's me or them.

Rachel McCormack: I'm going to learn how to make savoury steamed suet puddings, like steak and kidney. People in Spain think they sound disgusting. I want to go there and show them that they are glorious and that they should make them too.

Tim Hayward: I will obviously stop drinking. And give up meat and dairy and live a pure life. Also, I will stop lying.

Tim Anderson: I really need to stop eating things off the kitchen counter without first assessing what they are. Usually it's fine, but this has resulted in me eating cat food, and also something that I think was a bit of carbonised gunk that flaked off the gas ring.

Bakewell pudding

We've visited Bakewell twice and, on both occasions, leapt eagerly into discussing, and eating, its most famous export … the Bakewell tart. Or should that be pudding?

Let's start with the tart. It's the Bakewell baked good that most people are familiar with today. Small or large, it's made with shortcrust pastry spread with raspberry jam and a thick layer of almond frangipane – so, butter, sugar, ground almonds, egg and, usually, some almond extract to boost the flavour. That's baked, and then iced, and commercial versions usually feature a perky glacé cherry on top. That's the orthodoxy, anyway. Jordan Bourke suggests courting controversy and riffing around it, for example using hazelnuts instead of almonds, and replacing the jam with chocolate spread.

But Bakewell tart is a relative newcomer – a late nineteenth-century interloper on the scene – popular because it was easy to make and transported well, ideal for mass production. It didn't become well known until after the Second World War, as the burgeoning road network made the Peak District ever easier for tourists to get to, and the UK's sweet tooth peaked. If you want a true taste of Bakewell, opt for the older, and fiercely fought-over, Bakewell pudding.

'Whenever I hear the words 'invented by accident' attached to a recipe, I always have a slight warning bell. It's a bit of an insult to hard-working cooks in the past.' – Dr Annie Gray

Bakewell pudding is all over the town. Several places lay claim to its invention, usually an inn or hotel on the site, by a cook or tea-shop keeper who did … something. Mucked up a recipe or threw together a set of ingredients to produce a wonder – that kind of thing. **None of the stories ring true** for various reasons: the dates don't fit; the hostelry concerned had been demolished decades before; the people involved never met. What is certain is that there was a pudding in the eighteenth century, which was based on pastry, custard and a layer of preserves, candied peel or fruit. It was known by loads of different names, from alderman's pudding or sweetmeat pudding to a simple egg tart.

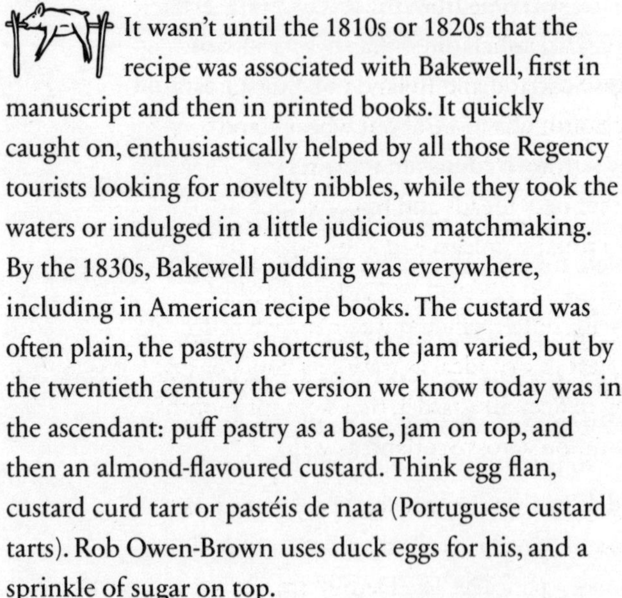

It wasn't until the 1810s or 1820s that the recipe was associated with Bakewell, first in manuscript and then in printed books. It quickly caught on, enthusiastically helped by all those Regency tourists looking for novelty nibbles, while they took the waters or indulged in a little judicious matchmaking. By the 1830s, Bakewell pudding was everywhere, including in American recipe books. The custard was often plain, the pastry shortcrust, the jam varied, but by the twentieth century the version we know today was in the ascendant: puff pastry as a base, jam on top, and then an almond-flavoured custard. Think egg flan, custard curd tart or pastéis de nata (Portuguese custard tarts). Rob Owen-Brown uses duck eggs for his, and a sprinkle of sugar on top.

'No icing. Definitely no cherries.' – Rob Owen-Brown

Oatcakes

All that talk of delicate sweet stuff may be making you crave a bit of something stodgier. Having successfully avoided being lynched when we suggested a chocolate Bakewell tart, we thought we'd settle an even weightier argument, and wade into the debate on oatcakes. Derbyshire is home to the Derbyshire oatcake, but our panel included Rob Owen-Brown, a staunch defender of the Staffie oatcake, and Jordan Bourke, speaking up for the Irish iteration.

The earliest recorded mentions of Derbyshire oatcakes come from the seventeenth century, but clearly they are much older than that. The North of England joins Scotland and Ireland in being an oats region – the South was more about wheat – and oatcakes are a strong tradition in every region. They are related to other oaty breads and biscuits, such as bannocks, all usually unleavened and cooked simply on a griddle stone. Irish oatcakes were originally just milled oats with butter, salt and water, mixed, rolled very flat and left to dry. Ideal as travellers' food, or just as something to keep in a larder, they kept for months, and were common across Scotland as well.

But back to the Derbyshire oatcake. It's a large, dark disc, made with oats, yeast and sometimes a little flour, and cooked like a pancake. The Derbyshire oatcake is bigger and thicker than those common in Staffordshire. Staffie oatcakes are more pliable, verging sometimes on the lacy, and lend themselves to being folded – never rolled – around things.

'I'd choose the Staffie oatcake, just because it's a lighter thing, almost like a crêpe, and it absorbs maple syrup very well. Anything that absorbs maple syrup, I like to eat.' – Rob Owen-Brown

When TKC visited Stoke-on-Trent, historian **Pamela Sambrook** explained that while Derbyshire oatcakes were cooked at home to feed hungry miners, the Staffie version quickly became a sort of cottage industry. Stoke was the heart of the British ceramics industry, which, along with male stokers and clay workers, employed a lot of women, working very long hours painting and finishing. They had neither time nor the energy to cook, and relied on oatcakes, sold through hatches and windows of the terraced houses that line Stoke's streets. Their makers were usually retired pottery workers who would do a roaring trade as people passed by and wanted breakfast, as oatcakes could also be hastily eaten at a workbench or heated up on a shovel in a kiln.

I think proper oatcakes – Staffie or Derbyshire – are amazing. But how do we elevate the humble oatcake? How can we make it a cultural icon?

While you can fill an oatcake with anything you can imagine, all of our panellists – and our audience – agreed that the classic, and best, combo was simply bacon and cheese. You can pimp oatcakes in all sorts of ways, but you risk moving them away from their roots, which is surely one of the reasons to celebrate them. Rachel McCormack reckons we need a wildly popular crime series, where the protagonist is heavily into oatcakes. She suggests taking inspiration from Manuel Vázquez Montalbán, a Spanish author whose Pepe Carvalho series was renowned for its gastronomic delights. The one dish it really boosted was the Catalan pa amb tomàquet (tomato bread). Montalbán was so revered for his food scenes that when Italian Andrea Camilleri decided to write about an equally food-obsessed detective, he paid homage to Montalbán and called his version Detective Montalbano. Fans hold Montalbano-themed banquets. Imagine that, but for oatcakes.

Lancashire oatcakes (yes, there are more) are different again, with no flour, so rougher and heftier. Rob Owen-Brown's recipe for a killer filling is as follows:

'Lancashire spring rolls', aka a filling for oatcakes

Sweat off some finely chopped leeks in plenty of butter – allow time and be careful not to burn them. Mix these with a bit of grain mustard, some diced cooked ham and a good amount of crumbled Lancashire cheese. Spread this mixture on your oatcakes and roll them round, tucking the ends in like a spring roll.

Dry January

Time, now, to move beyond Bakewell, and into the wider climes of January. As we recover from our Christmas indulgence and take down the decorations, many of us will be making food resolutions, and, as ever, we're here to help.

For lots of people Dry January has become a thing. Invented in 2013 by Alcohol Change UK, it quickly became a popular way to change habits and tackle drinking culture. Whatever people's motivation – to check they can give up the booze, to kick start permanent change, to begin the year with a challenge, or as part of a wider health kick – its popularity has grown year on year, and it's fair to say that even if you aren't doing it, you'll know someone who is. But it's easy to panic at the end of a long day, when usually you'd reach for a glass of wine, and every year we get questions on how to give our brains the signal to switch off, without falling off the wagon.

This year we've decided to try going dry in January. But we still want to have something nice to drink in the evening. Can the panel recommend something to plug the gap?

First up, how about a classic mocktail, an alcohol-free version of a set of drinks with a notoriously flexible relationship with a sensible ABV? Tim Hayward opts for a Virgin Mary, a vodka-free Bloody Mary, just tomato juice, salt, Tabasco or other hot sauce, and a stick of celery. To replicate the kick of vodka, try adding horseradish.

If you want to make soft drinks more fun, add fizz. Dr Zoe Laughlin says theatricality in presentation is always a winner. Many juices and cordials are acid, so just add an alkali and stand back. A ¼ teaspoon bicarbonate of soda will give a glorious effect – not long-lasting, but if it's between that and adding vodka, a sudden wild fizzing is a real crowd-pleaser. It's especially good if you add it to a shrub – a drinking vinegar.

Angela Hartnett suggests looking to cultures with a long history of teetotalism. She recommends Saudi champagne, made from fresh apple juice, fizzy water and ginger. Make it special by dipping the glass in liquid and then sugar to get a sugared rim. You can use water, honey or orange juice for the liquid, and dip simply in plain sugar, but even better is a mixture of sugar, cinnamon and a pinch of salt. Finish by scattering a few rose petals on top.

There's a history of teetotalism in British culture too. The Temperance movement had its roots in the late eighteenth-century Methodist movement, whose founder, John Wesley, urged its members to forgo alcohol and drink tea instead. He, and later social reformers, promoted Temperance among the working classes as a way of saving money, encouraging good health and avoiding vice and violence. In 1833 the Preston Temperance Society became the first official Temperance society and it was in the minutes of one of their meetings that the word teetotal was first recorded. The early movement spawned a large number of other societies, members of which 'took the pledge'. Annie Gray suggests anyone looking for Dry January suggestions from the past should head to a book called *Temperance Drinks*, published in 1904. In it you can find recipes for oat milk, various 'ades' (lemon, orange and ginger) and 'a famous drink', which is basically barley water. There are also shrubs and a zingy peppermint and ginger cordial.

Near Manchester, you can find the UK's last remaining Temperance bar, Fitzpatrick's. It still sells cordials and hot toddies inspired by the original movement. Many of the herbal drinks, such as dandelion and burdock or sarsaparilla (similar to root beer and derived from the sassafras plant), date back to the 1840s and were originally marketed on (often slightly spurious) health grounds.

Cordials started out in the late sixteenth century as medicinal drinks. Most were highly alcoholic distillations – gin was a cordial, as was schnapps. By the seventeenth century, they were drunk as much for pleasure as to cure pains. But the association with health endured, and the word was adopted by the Temperance movement. They used it purely for non-alcoholic beverages, seeking to show that alcohol-free didn't mean devoid of interest. Fruit cordials could be made with jam – the sugar and fruit making a proto fruit squash – and mixed with carbonated water for a bit of jazz. Meanwhile, herbal infusions were not only cheap but carried that all-important air of goodness about them. They weren't just sold in specialist bars or made at home, either. Vimto, founded in 1908, is one brand that is still around today, but which started out as a herbal tonic. The name is a portmanteau of 'vim' and 'tonic'. In 1938, Ribena was also first marketed for health.

However, fruit squashes aren't exactly joyful for a novice setting out on Dry January. Not, that is, until you heat them up.

What's a good alternative to mulled wine? I love a big winter gathering, but not everyone drinks, and lots of us have kids. What can I make that is both warming and welcoming?

Rob Owen-Brown favours cooking with heavily fruited, punchy cordials and infamously once put a Vimto trifle on one of his menus. He suggests using a dark, rich fruit drink as a base for a dry version of mulled wine, and oomphing it up with spices and herbs. You can use all of the spices you'd associate with alcoholic mulled wine – cinnamon, ginger, cloves, mace, allspice and nutmeg – but also throw in a sprig or three of rosemary and some juniper to add a bitter back note. If it's for a party, make it in a huge pan, and hang orange peel all round it to add a festive air.

Apple juice also mulls well and makes a lighter alternative, ideal for those who prefer mulled white wine. Or try making wassail, traditionally drunk at Twelfth Night to bring luck for the harvest. You can easily make it with a non-alcoholic beer, simmered with spices and a bit of cream. For a Victorian twist, core but don't peel some apples, keeping them whole. Fill the centres with a bit of brown sugar and roast them until they are really soft before putting them at the bottom of your serving bowl. Everyone then digs in with a ladle. Your aim is to fill your mug with a dollop of squidgy caramelised apple and some spicy, creamy hot beer. You could, of course, try heating it with a poker, red hot from the fire, but that may be going a little too far.

Finally, those of you with blenders could try going down the smoothie route – though Prof. Peter Barham adds a cautionary note about any whiff of the word detox.

'There's no such thing as a detox diet – just drink plenty of water and let your kidneys do their work.' – Peter Barham

But a smoothie can be a good substitute for a beer or another long drink. If you don't add sugar, and favour flavours such as ginger and turmeric, it will stop it from becoming too much like a child's breakfast drink, and mean you are more likely to savour it, rather than neck it all in one go.

Panellist pick: *Food in films*

We're united in choosing the Pixar-animated *Ratatouille* as one of our favourite films. No spoilers here: if you haven't watched it, you are in for a treat. Jay Rayner agrees, adding that apart from the hair, he's always tried to model himself just a little bit on food critic Anton Ego with his trusty notepad. Also, according to one audience member, Remy, the film's central character, sounds just like Tim Anderson.

Other top picks include the 1987 homage to high Victorian haute cuisine, *Babette's Feast*; and Jon Favreau's unassuming indie film *Chef*, which is full of big-name cameos, all of whom play second fiddle to the food.

Top tip: ***Peeling ginger with a teaspoon***

Struggling to get into the cracks and crevices of a ginger root with your conventional peeler or paring knife? Sophie Wright was amazed we didn't know the knack. She uses a teaspoon, simply running the tip of the spoon over the root to easily scrape off the peel. The fibres don't get caught in the peeler, your knives don't get blunt, and you can do a whole root in seconds. She showed us. Some of us haven't stopped talking about it since.

Top tip: ***Wrapping herbs***

Another one of Sophie's tips is around making the best of your bags of supermarket herbs. With the exception of coriander, which will wilt and go brown as soon as you look at it, you can extend the life of your bunches to well over a week. Just remove them from the packet and wrap the ends firmly in wetted kitchen roll. Slide the bunch back into the plastic (or use a well-washed bag) and keep them in the fridge. For coriander though, there's no hope. Best buy it ready-frozen or grow your own.

Feel free to scribble any recipe notes below …

Citrus fruits

Oranges are one of the key flavours at the moment, and very lovely they are too (see December). But they really aren't the only fruit ... let's pucker up and turn our tastebuds to the slightly less obvious side of citrus.

There's a lot to love about the many faces of citrus. We're still deep into satsuma season, along with all their little orange-y cousins: clementines, tangerines, tangelos – the list goes on. For many of us, just the sight of them brings a true Proustian rush. But why do we get such a visceral hit from a simple piece of fruit? Prof. Charles Spence says we aren't imagining it. Food aromas go straight to the emotional centres of the brain, evoking all the memories of mandarins past, and plunging us back, in some cases, to our childhoods, and all the associations thereof. As children we seem to love a bit of sour. If you give a baby a piece of lemon to suck on, the baby will take it, suck on it, and then spit it out with an expression of pure horror. But then it'll go back for more. We seem to be addicted to the 'ouch-but yes' sensation of sharp, sour citrus from a really young age. It isn't surprising that we all have memories of citrussy flavours from our childhood, or that citrus finds its way into so many things.

For the Japanese, citrus is a vital part of a traditional New Year's delicacy called kagami mochi. Looking like a flattened snowman, it's made from two white glutinous rice cakes (mochi) stacked on top of each other and topped with a small citrus fruit called a daidai (Japanese bitter orange). Daidai can be written in such a way as to mean 'generations', and it is very symbolic.

Satsumas also have a Japanese link, for they are named for the former southern Japanese province, present-day Kagoshima. In Japan, they are not known by this name; there, they are called mikan, simply the word for mandarin oranges.

Tim Anderson says his grandma used to make a salad with satsumas, roasted pecans and any type of leaf she could find, which goes fantastically with wafu dressing. Wafu dressing is a catch-all term for 'Japanese-style' salad dressings based mainly on soy sauce. There are many variations. A simple version is made with equal parts soy sauce, rice vinegar, mirin, plus grated onion (or shallot) and ginger. Some versions contain oil, some do not.

We always have loads of clementines and things like that left over from Christmas. Apart from eating them, or using them to decorate the top of a retro cheesecake, what else can I cook with them?

As lovely as they are as a decoration, Sophie Wright says clementines are as good in the cake as on top of it. She suggests a winter warmer riff on a lemon drizzle cake:

Spiced clementine cake

You can use mandarins, clementines or tangerines for this. Start with 6 clementines (about 500g). Just cover them in water, add 50g sugar and spice. Sophie uses a bay leaf, ½ a star anise, 3 cloves and ½ a cinnamon stick. Simmer them for about 2 hours until they are really soft, and just starting to burst. Remove the seeds as you see them. Then blitz them whole, all the pith and everything. Add 6 eggs and 175g sugar and beat until light and fluffy. Now fold in 250g ground almonds and a teaspoon of baking powder. Turn into a 20cm round tin and bake at 170°C for around an hour (you may want to cover the top halfway through if it starts to brown). Meanwhile, reduce your boiling liquid to about two-thirds and leave it to cool. Get the cake out of the oven and, while it's still hot, make holes in it with a skewer and pour your syrup over it. It's absolutely delicious served with a spoonful of crème fraîche.

You can also use a wide range of citrus to cure fish, as an alternative or addition to the lemons and limes we're familiar with in ceviches and related dishes. How about Hawaiian poke (pronounced pokey), which is just chunks of very fresh raw fish, marinated in soy sauce, sesame oil, lime juice and zest, clementine juice and zest, a bit of chilli and some spring onion? Add macadamia nuts and sesame seeds to make a sort of sashimi salad.

Or go with gravadlax. Andi Oliver does hers with salt, a little sugar, some pink peppercorns and mandarin juice and zest, wrapped up tightly in plastic wrap (or its equivalent) and left in the fridge for a couple of days.

If all this talk of easy peelers makes you turn a bit sour, fear not. There's an almost infinite variety of citrus fruit, though they all come from just four (possibly five) ancestral species: the small-flowered papeda, the citron, the pomelo and the mandarin.

(Some scientists add the kumquat, too.) Almost all citrus can cross-pollinate, producing offspring with characteristics drawn from both parent trees. Through centuries of wild and selective breeding, we now have hundreds of forms, mainly drawn from just citrons, pomelos and mandarins. Want an example? How about a grapefruit, which comes from a pomelo and a sweet orange. The sweet orange is in turn a relation of the mandarin. The sour orange is also a descendant of the mandarin, which when crossed with a citron gives us … a lemon. This is heavily simplified, but you get the general picture.

Citrus fruits are native to South and East Asia and, while there is a lot of debate about which fruits originated when and where, lemons seem to have been grown ornamentally by the Romans, and oranges were the subject of a detailed monograph from twelfth-century China. By the Renaissance, they were becoming big business in Italy, and it was in the gardens of the Italian nobility that many of the varieties we still know today were first bred. Groves of sweetly scented citrus trees were familiar sights in many villas, and the flowers were used for perfume as well as flavouring custards and cakes.

Citron was probably one of the earliest types of citrus in the UK, but we've barely heard of it now. We all eat it though – it's the main ingredient in mixed candied peel.

One of the coolest-looking types of citrus is Buddha's hand, a type of lime. Tim Anderson buys it whenever he can but warns that it has virtually no juice. However, it does have incredibly fragrant zest. He's also a huge fan of yuzu, which he describes as a mixture of lemon, lime, grapefruit and a bit of spruce pine. It's heavily used in both Japanese and Korean cookery. Kumquats, too, are worth seeking out – eat them as they are, no need to peel, or preserve them as you would lemons, sliced open and packed full of salt.

Ever wondered why the British were once called 'limeys'? It's all about scurvy and the hunt for a cure. We may only have discovered vitamins in the twentieth century, but people were dying of vitamin deficiency for a very long time before that. Scurvy – vitamin C deficiency – was a problem from the fifteenth century onwards and became really very urgent as global sea travel increased and, with it, long sea voyages with no fresh food on board. Every country was after a solution – the Chinese carried fresh ginger plants on their ships – and the English carried out all sorts of experiments to try and find a cure. Eventually, they hit upon lemons. But lemons were expensive, so they switched to limes (which, unfortunately, aren't as high in vitamin C) instead. Hence British sailors became known as limeys.

I like the idea of limes, but when I buy them they just sit around until they go brown and I have to throw them out. What can I do with them that is easy and doesn't need loads of extra ingredients?

We tend to associate limes with Asian cookery. Lemon is a much more dominant flavour in western European cookery. But Rachel McCormack says we should be a bit braver. South American cooks use lemon and lime more interchangeably. So, try it in something as British-feeling as a fish pie, replacing the lemon zest with lime zest, and serving it with a wedge of lime.

Tim Anderson suggests a simple lime-peel pickle, made by fermenting lime peel, salt, soy sauce, chilli and a bit of sugar for a week or so until the bitterness melts away and the peel is delightfully soft. But steer clear of blood oranges, which he sees as a gimmick. Small, pippy and pointless. Opt for bergamot, finger limes and pomelos instead.

Cheese: *Before or after dessert?*

In the blue corner is **Annie Gray**, who is firmly in favour of eating before. She says the whole confusion comes from the change from *à la Française* to *à la Russe* eating in the late nineteenth century. Under an *à la Française* meal, you'd have two courses – each of many dishes – followed by dessert, which was just fruit, nuts, delicate biscuits to dunk in your wine, and exquisite sugary things. The second course also had sweet things though, heavier things, like puddings and tarts – served at the same time as the roasts. If you ate cheese, it came between the hefty sweet things of the second course, and the more frivolous things of dessert. It was supposed to cleanse the palate and prepare it for dessert and dessert wines. Then as times changed, and meals got smaller, different countries ended up with sweet things and cheese in different places. But Annie learnt to love food when she lived briefly in France, and feels for both historical and practical reasons, they've got it right.

In the green corner is **Tim Hayward**, who normally has to be forcibly separated from Annie whenever this topic arises. He says having a poncy little dessert and pushing off to bed is fine for the French, but he is with the British way with cheese. End the meal, push it all aside, break out a wedge of salty cheese and a great big bottle of port, and just keep going. Four hours later, everyone is utterly ripped and debating politics and science and the night is still young.

And lastly, a cautionary tale from an audience member from the show in Stockwell, London.

'Our most disturbing breakfast ever was on our first day in Krakow when, while enjoying coffee and pastries, we realised we were in a brothel.

'We went with about a week's notice and we couldn't find the hotel we were booked into. So, the taxi driver from the airport took us to his brother's hotel, which we thought was marvellous. We got there quite late and settled in and it was … quite lively. And then the next morning we got up, and we were sitting there sipping coffee, and realised that there were two price boards up. One for rooms by the hour and the other, clearly more rarely consulted, for our overnight rate.'

Oops.

February

Things to get excited about this month:

Chinese New Year (2022 is the Year of the Tiger. Suitably symbolic foods include nian gao – glutinous rice cakes – for success, and fish for prosperity)

Wakefield Rhubarb Festival (little pink stems of joy)

Great British Beer Festival Winter (formerly the CAMRA Winter Ales Festival. Celebrate the stout!)

Valentine's Day (need we elaborate? We do, further on …)

Rye Bay Scallop Week

National Toast Day (and butter, obviously)

The Oscars (Films! Food! Why not?)

Collop Monday (the day before Shrove Tuesday … time to eat all the meat before Lent kicks in)

The moon this month is made of **St James**

Early spring is the time for quickly produced, barely aged cheeses made with milk from the new season's births. That often means cream or curd cheeses, but St James is a sheep's milk washed-rind cheese, which goes from sheep to shop in just over a month. Production stops when the milk stops in early autumn. An ideal gateway cheese into soft, stinky, more challenging washed-rind types.

This month *The Kitchen Cabinet* is in **York**, known for its Vikings, its medieval Minster and as the former centre for the UK's chocolate industry.

Key flavours this month include **winter turnips**, **forced rhubarb**, the last of this year's fresh **game** and last year's **maincrop potatoes**.

And we are also thinking about:

- The best way to fake luxury at the dinner table
- How to occupy children at half-term
- Valentine's gifts
- Keeping the bubbles in the bottle
- And the best way to cook an omelette

Welcome to York, a city with a rich history of eating and drinking, where every cobble covers layers of evidence of what came before.

Known as Eboracum to the Romans, Eoforwick to the Saxons and Jorvik to the Vikings, York has been a centre for governing and gallivanting since the first century. Strolling its streets will bring you up close and personal with every era of architecture, from its medieval city walls to the Grade II-listed taxi kiosk some of us noticed as we spilled out from the station. We were a little distracted though – catch it on a good day and the whole city smells of chocolate – an olfactory reminder of York's chocolate heritage. And yes, it is indeed where the Yorkie was born.

Top tip: *Fake it to make it*

We all have certain friends to whom we just want to show off a little bit. Prof. Charles Spence has you covered. He suggests that if you are serving pre-dinner drinks, especially if it is a sherry, G&T or something of that ilk, pick a really heavy glass. It doesn't have to be expensive, just heavy. When we looked at how much people thought their gins cost, the gins served in flimsy glassware universally came out as cheaper than those served in something with a thick bottom and a real heft.

Herring

York is particularly renowned for its Viking heritage, and is the home of the Jorvik Viking Centre, where you can not only see the various archaeological finds from the many digs over the decades, but also smell what Viking York was like (poo and apples, in case you were wondering).

York became a Viking city after being besieged by the wonderfully named King Halfden and Ivar the Boneless in 866. The city became part of the Danelaw, an area under Viking rule that stretched from Chester through to Bedford and down to London. Far from ushering in a fashion for horned helmets and pillaging, the Vikings in fact settled down, married locals and adapted their native foods to their new home.

Archaeological evidence reveals a diet rich in beef, mutton and pork. However, the Vikings were also very keen on fish, especially herring, which they smoked and salted.

But what exactly is herring? Or, rather, what isn't it? **David Herford**, who was on our Dartmouth show, explained that people get mixed up. 'They think a whitebait grows into a sprat and it doesn't, it's a totally different species.' And a sprat doesn't grow into a herring and a herring definitely doesn't grow into a mackerel. They are all different species, but they are related (whitebait are completely different, and are the young of lots of different species). As ever, we'd recommend checking for an MSC blue label to be

sure that the fish you choose is sustainable – currently mackerel are pretty good, and whitebait to be avoided.

Herring is an underused fish in the UK today, but was very popular in the past. Paula McIntyre uses freshwater herrings from Lough Neagh, trapped in the waters of the lake during the last ice age and known as silver darlings. She recommends a traditional Ulster recipe, also very common in Scotland.

Herring in oatmeal

Ideally use herring fillets for this. All you do is cover them in pinhead oatmeal (not rolled oats). Heat some bacon fat in a pan, fry off your herring – it doesn't matter if the oatmeal falls off a bit. Serve it with potato farls and, to make it even better, add crispy bits of bacon.

Fresh herring go off fast. But, like any oily fish, they are ideal for salting and smoking and were once widely used as a food to preserve for the winter. Food preservation methods in the past were all based on just a few scientific principles, which aimed to stop the bacteria growing. Prof. Peter Barham says it's really quite simple: you either remove the water (drying) or replace it with something salty or acidic (salting, pickling). As a final step, you can also introduce a toxin (smoking).

Oily fish lend themselves to all this much better than white fish, which become very dry. Dried cod – stockfish – was notorious for needing days of soaking to soften it enough to become edible, facilitated by hitting it with a mallet.

Herring had other advantages too: they were easy to spot at sea due to gannets swooping on the shoals as they surfaced, and they were both plentiful and cheap. For poor Victorians, they were a staple food, and they were then by far the most landed catch (by weight) in British ports.

The vast majority were smoked, usually having first been salted for good measure. In the 1840s in Northumberland, a new type of curing process was pioneered, quickly becoming the dominant form of cured herring in the UK: the smoked kipper. They were tasty and easy to transport on the shiny new railway network, and different towns developed their own specific curing methods. Craster, the Isle of Man and Mallaig in Scotland all became famous for the quality of their kippering.

My partner loves nothing better on a Sunday morning than to cook up a kipper. Has the panel any advice on how I can either stop him doing this or just stop the smell?

When we were in Newcastle, we asked our audience how they liked their kippers. Turns out you are a traditional lot – 55% thrilling to the simplicity of hot kippers on well-buttered toast. But you're also partial to using them as part of a resolutely savoury afternoon tea. However, that leaves around 20% of you really preferring them back in the sea.

The smell is lessened if you poach them in milk, but Rachel McCormack admits that a true kipper aficionado won't have any of that: it is grilling or nothing. The best she can suggest is to get some bacon going at the same time. Go smelly or go home. That said, there are kippers and there are kippers. It's worth getting the good stuff, from a proper smokehouse, preferably one blackened with tar and with a waft that knocks you out at a hundred paces. Traditional cures go heavy on real smoke rather than smoke flavour but easy on the dye.

'It honks. Really, truly, honks. But stinky isn't always bad. In food terms, stinky can be sublime.' – Jay Rayner

If you're not keen on strong, fishy smells, count yourself lucky that the British herring is simply kippered. The most famous Scandinavian twist on herring is surströmming. This tends to come in tins and is lightly salted and then fermented. The name comes from the Baltic herring, 'strömming' in Swedish, and it is known as one of world's smelliest foods. Jay Rayner tried some once (search online for 'Jay Rayner surströmming'). His reaction went along the lines of, 'It's all right … bit armpitty … oh God, FAECES,' then his eyes started watering. However, in the name of science, gluttony and not being chicken, he ate some. The verdict? Appalling, but also deeply compelling. The Swedes pair it with things like potatoes, crème fraîche, red onion, perhaps some Västerbottensost (hard cheese, a bit like a pecorino or manchego) and tunnbröd (a wheat and rye flatbread), making for what Prof. Barry Smith calls synergistic umami, when two umami-rich foods come together to make a glorious whole.

Chocolate

There's nowhere to go once you've started on foods that pair well with the smell of armpits, so let's head in the opposite direction, to one of the most evocative smells in the gastronomic playbook.

Another of York's claims to food fame is its strong links to the chocolate industry. In 1725, Mary Tuke, a Quaker, set up a small shop on York's Walmgate, inadvertently making history. For this small beginning was the start of a chocolate-making tradition that for a long time helped to define the city. Sadly, the Terry's factory closed in 2005, while Rowntree's is now part of Nestlé.

The history of chocolate is much longer than that of the factories that produced it. *Theobroma cacao*, the cacao or cocoa tree, is native to South and Central America, where chocolate was widely used by the Mayans and Aztecs. They consumed it as a cold drink, made with water, thickened with maize and spiced. When the Spanish invaded South America, they brought chocolate back to the Old World, where it eventually gained popularity as a hot drink, usually with milk.

Gradually, people started to cook with it, in blancmanges, creams, custards, ice creams and sorbets, and in the nineteenth century chocolate bars started to debut, as well as chocolate-coated confectionery. But they were all based on dark chocolate. Firms like those in York, plus Cadbury's in Birmingham and Fry's in Bristol, all capitalised on the market for drinking chocolate and cocoa powder. The market for eating chocolate was tiny in comparison. For anything approaching modern eating chocolate, eager eaters had to wait until the last quarter of the nineteenth century, when milk chocolate was developed in Switzerland. Once invented, however, its rise was meteoric.

In the audience in York was **Richard Pollitt**, curator of York's Mansion House. He came clutching a small metal box, emblazoned with flags and the York coat of arms. Inside, a bar of chocolate that celebrated its centenary in 2014. In 1914, the then Mayor and Sheriff sent a bar of Rowntree's chocolate to every combatant and non-combatant from York. They ended up all over the world. This one eventually came back, intact, and is now part of the collection Richard looks after. We did ask, and yes, it does still smell distinctly of chocolate.

I've just come back from Barcelona, where I had the best hot chocolate I've ever drunk. But I can't find anything like it in the UK, and I don't seem to be able to replicate it at home. Help!

February is the coldest month, so the idea of a warming hot chocolate has a certain appeal. Dr Annie Gray's favourite recipe is from the 1650s and is simply dark chocolate with milk, ground almonds, orange flower water and a blend of chilli, cinnamon, aniseed and cloves. It should be whisked with a special tool, a molinillo, but a whisk will do. She says it's the dish that made her fall in love with food history.

Sophie Wright also favours spice, with a delicious Malaysian hot chocolate made from cinnamon, cardamom, 75% chocolate and condensed milk. You can also add a pinch of black tea for bitterness or swap the condensed milk for whole milk or coconut milk. It's a riff on teh tarik, pulled tea, which is traditionally poured from a great height to get a good froth on top and is sweet, silky and, as one audience member sighed as she tried it, 'beautiful'. If that sounds a bit too risky for the kitchen floor, Sophie recommends cheating by adding a spoonful of Horlicks or a similar malted drink to your basic chocolate mixture with a pinch of salt and some cinnamon.

Choosing the right chocolate is crucial. Cocoa powder just won't do it for a really smooth, creamy hot chocolate. Rachel McCormack says for a true Barcelona-style chocolate caliente, always use actual chocolate. She uses the darkest she can get and adjusts the sweetness afterwards. Use whole milk, never low fat, and, for the ultimate thick mix, add a teaspoon of cornflour (mixed with the milk while cold). Andi Oliver goes one better and squirts cream over and tops it with a flake.

'I promised recipes, I didn't promise class. But it's really good.' – Andi Oliver

The question of what type of chocolate to use for drinking, cooking and eating is quite personal. Dr Zoe Laughlin would like you to try a quick experiment. Take two pieces of chocolate, one at 70% cocoa solids and one good milk chocolate. Put the dark one in your mouth and hold it there. Don't chew! Let it dissolve. Good, right? Now do the same for the milk. You'll find that it melts more quickly and seems to carry flavour faster. It's all to do with the percentages of milk solids and cocoa butter. She prefers milk for eating and dark for cooking, because one is designed for maximum mouth-meltability and the other … isn't.

This is also why you shouldn't keep chocolate in the fridge – it defeats the very point of all that careful food science (plus the sugar structure breaks down and it can 'bloom' and lose its lovely shine).

Barry Smith adds that texture is also really important. The brain interprets smoothness as sweetness, so if you love chocolate but want to cut down on sugar, go for one that is high in cocoa solids but as finely ground as you can get it.

I'm keen to use chocolate in savoury cooking, but I don't know where to start. Any tips?

Dark chocolate makes an excellent ingredient for savoury dishes, though unsweetened chocolate is surprisingly bitter. So, don't go full-on 100% cocoa solids, use something around 70%.

Andi Oliver has been perfecting her curry goat for about 20 years. She refuses to divulge the recipe, despite repeated begging, but says it is approaching perfection. The secret is about five squares of 80% to 90% chocolate in a pot of curried goat, which would normally feed 10.

Sue Lawrence uses it in mole poblano, the dark, rich sauce that has become iconic in Mexican cookery. There's no single recipe; every family has their own version. It's a real hybrid, mixing native ingredients, such as chilli and tomatoes, with Old World spices such as cinnamon. Many recipes use chocolate, a native ingredient but one that was not cooked with until the creolisation of Mexican cuisine as Spanish influence grew stronger. Sue says it's great with poultry.

Rob Owen-Brown, meanwhile, uses it to boost his stewed red cabbage:

Red cabbage with chocolate

Mince ½ Scotch bonnet and 2 red onions. Sweat them down in butter until they're nice and caramelised, then add ½ red cabbage, chopped, and cook it down. Give it an hour or so until it forms a really sticky mess, adding a little beef or venison stock if it starts to burn. Finally, grate about 30–50g dark chocolate over it. The cabbage is excellent with a venison steak.

Chocolate also has a real affinity with salt, while umami-rich flavours like soy really boost sweetness. Try Tim Anderson's chilli chocolate cornflake squares, boosted with Japanese shichimi powder, which is not just chilli, but also ginger, orange peel, seaweed and sesame. He says they are even better made with pork scratchings.

Chilli and chocolate are a running theme. Barry Smith points out that the two have a very long association and share certain characteristics. As well as being New World ingredients that we've really taken into our hearts (or kitchens, which is the same thing on TKC) both were seen as aphrodisiacs. They were touted as a cure for impotence and as a guaranteed way to bring some sweet loving into lacklustre lives.

Panellist pick: *Food fun for half-term*

Desperate for something both time-consuming but practical, with a definite risk of an almighty mess but a real payoff if it all goes well? Make your own butter. Zoe Laughlin does it in a stand mixer, Annie Gray has a 1950s butter churn, but you can also make it by shaking it in a (tightly lidded) jam jar. Just take double cream, at room temperature, and churn it until the butter separates from the buttermilk. It should go clunk (and can take up to 45 minutes). Rinse it well, and then squeeze out the buttermilk with a couple of flat spatulas on a big chopping board (put a cloth underneath the board to catch the liquid). Salt or flavour as you fancy. Eat it quickly though – home-made butter goes all sorts of interesting colours after a few days.

Top tip: *Keeping the fizz in the bottle*

As unlikely as it is that you'd still have some champagne in the bottle, what happens if you want to keep it for the next day? We've all heard that stashing it back in the fridge with a spoon in the top will do it. But Peter Barham says it has nothing to do with the spoon, and everything to do with the solubility of gas in liquid, which is greater at low temperatures. Your fridge should be below 5°C, and at that temperature the carbon dioxide will stay dissolved in the alcohol in the fizz regardless of what's sticking out of the top.

Panellist pick: *Romantic gifts for the greedy*

Chocolates are all fine and dandy, but what can you buy for the true gourmand in your life? How about a love-themed cookbook? Tim Hayward recommends Norman Douglas's delightfully absurd *Venus in the Kitchen*, which is replete with recipes for flagging elderly libidos. But it's Rachel McCormack that we always look to on this topic. She claims not to have a romantic bone in her body, but she is also the proud owner of the extremely pink *Romance of Food* by novelist Barbara Cartland. There are copious cupids on the front cover. Rachel also recommends *Aphrodite* by Isabel Allende, whose advice is essentially that no-one under the age of 40 needs anything more than camomile tea to get them going anyway, so presents or pink food are pointless. If the relationship is right, whatever you do is intrinsically loving.

Valentine's Day

If the thought of that is getting you all hot under the collar, well, yes, we'd be shirking our duties bringing culinary advice to the nation if we let February go past without getting into the food of lurve.

Let's not beat about the bush. Time to go to the big question on everybody's lips. Aphrodisiacs. Are they real?

Peter Barham says sadly not. There's very little science to support the idea of a universal food to charge the loins and fire the heart. There are a few foods with a bit of potential, including chilli, which brings an endorphin rush. But the idea that heat in the mouth sends heat further down just isn't true. Then there's chocolate, which contains the stimulant theobromine – but in minuscule quantities.

'The link with chocolate and sex started early: there's a brilliant seventeenth-century ditty that includes the line, "Twill make old women young and fresh, create new notions of the flesh, and cause them to yearn for you-know-what, if they but taste of chocolate".' – Annie Gray

Some of its modern appeal may just be associative. Food has the ability to spark memories like little else. So, if chocolate – or anything else – triggers sexy memories, then it is an aphrodisiac. **Don't underestimate the power of an urban myth**, either. Chocolate was being touted as a sex aid within decades of its introduction, so it is no wonder we believe there might be a basis in fact, when there really isn't.

Chocolate's not the only food with a long association with sex. A lot of so-called aphrodisiacs were (or are) very expensive – saffron, gold leaf, truffles, champagne – and sex helps sell them. Some foods got a reputation due to a medical theory called the Doctrine of Signatures, which held that foods contained physical indications as to the effect they would have on the body. Anything that was red or looked a bit like a heart would affect the blood and might therefore incite lust while, more importantly, anything that looked a bit like genitalia would (obviously) have an immediate effect on the relevant part. Thus, oysters were great because they looked like female genitalia (use your imagination), stinkhorn mushrooms were perfect (the Latin name *Phallus impudicus* says it all), and roots like that of sea holly (eryngo) were also held in high regard. It was a pretty universal concept. The word avocado comes from the Nahuatl word 'āhuacatl', which is a slang term for testicle. Avocados, you've guessed it, have also been used as aphrodisiacs.

I always find restaurants a bit much on Valentine's Day. What can I cook to convince myself and my partner that staying in is the new going out?

Actual testicles were also supposed to be aphrodisiacs – the euphemistically named lamb's stones, for example, – and there's a whole host of foods, such as sows' nipples, vulvas and womb, which aren't exactly common on modern menus. You could try serving them to your loved one – the Roman cookery writer Apicius will be very helpful here – but perhaps it's best to put all thoughts of aphrodisiacs to bed and concentrate on food to woo in other ways. We can't really advise on exactly what will float your individual boats so, instead, how about learning from our mistakes?

Sue Lawrence advises that you don't do a new recipe for the first time without the major ingredients. While a student, she splashed out on grouse, intending to roast them on whisky-soaked thyme, but a heady mix of cost and availability meant she ended up swapping the thyme for heather from a nearby rockery and the whisky for kirsch. Safe to say, the flavour profiles were a little bit different. Plus, when she opened the oven, it was to a waft of weedkiller. Safe to say romance quickly died.

Don't pick random stuff from the roadside. The tang of fumes and spatter of dog really isn't an appetite enhancer.

Rob Owen-Brown, meanwhile, strongly suggests checking what the subject of your culinary courting actually likes. He once slow-cooked a pig's head in prune sauce – an immensely time-consuming dish involving shaving the head and dewaxing the ears. He was very proud. She called him a devil and 'disappeared in a puff of perfume and a little black dress.'

He should have cooked it for Tim Hayward, who says one of the most romantic cooking experiences he's ever had was with Fergus Henderson. They cooked a half pig's head together in Henderson's restaurant, St. John, talking, drinking and breathing in the heady aroma of piggy goodness. Fergus said watching couples share the final dish was intensely romantic. Tim said if he wasn't already married, he might just have proposed.

Finally, a word on what to wear. Make sure you can move. Here's Sophie Wright on a second date:

'So, I put on a pair of leather trousers, which I hadn't sat down in yet, and we're at the bar, me and this tall, dark, handsome man, and I'm looking at our table with these low metal chairs thinking, I'm never going to get down into that. And I didn't. I spent the whole meal hovered over this chair and my thighs were burning. Eventually, I just had to sit down and, of course, I popped my zip and the button ended up in his lap.'

Happily, they were several bottles down and, guess what? Reader, she married him.

The best way to cook an omelette?

We've never quite come to blows on this, but it's a close-run thing, and it comes up a lot in our postbag. All of us agree that the fast-cooked omelette is a horror: low and slow is your friend. Aim for a 7-minute omelette, never a 3. Nearly all of us favour a heavy-bottomed non-stick pan, though lots of butter is also helpful. Jocky Petrie blends and sieves his eggs for the perfect texture, and it really does work. Keep the eggs moving until they are nearly done, and then stop – the top should still be just a little bit runny. And get it out fast – nobody likes a tepid omelette.

Pancakes

If all of that has you salivating for something simpler, how about a meal for one with no jeopardy involved? Hoorah! For February also brings an excuse for one of the simplest foods around. Flat, rolled, sweet, savoury – it's time to celebrate the humble, but delicious, pancake.

Cooking on a stone or metal plate is older than ovens, and one of the most ancient and universal ways to cook. It's unsurprising that pancakes exist in nearly every culture, even if they aren't always called that. Most western countries have a day devoted to them – sometimes Shrove Tuesday, sometimes Candlemas – which is linked to the religious calendar, but pancakes really aren't just for Pancake Day.

I recently tried a chickpea pancake. It was amazing and now I'm wondering if I've been missing out my whole life by thinking of them as just an eggy batter, mainly for kids?

If you need convincing to explore the wider world of pancakes, you need only nip across the Channel and into a crêperie. Originally a Breton institution, which spread out to cater for migrating workers, there are around 5000 crêperies in France and they are spreading globally, fast. The wheat-based basic crêpe isn't that different to the batter-based British pancake, but the French use it purely for sweet toppings. For a savoury punch, you can't beat a buckwheat galette.

Jordan Bourke is an aficionado of a different French pancake. Originally from Italy, socca is a chickpea pancake that has become emblematic of Nice. Depending on where you eat it, it's also called panisse or farinata.

Socca (farinata)

If you can get chickpea (gram) flour, great, otherwise you can grind dried chickpeas (they need to be very fine, like flour, something best done in a coffee or spice grinder in small batches). Just mix about 250g chickpea flour with 500ml sparkling water, 3 or 4 tablespoons olive oil and sea salt. Pour about 3 tablespoons of olive oil into a large frying pan (non-stick or well-seasoned cast iron) and add enough batter to thickly cover the base – you need it to be about ½cm thick. Fry over a high heat until it begins to dry out on the surface, then flip and fry for another 30 seconds. In Nice it's just served with lots of black pepper, but Jordan loves it with finely chopped olives, parsley and red onion, plus sea salt and a bit of extra-virgin olive oil drizzled over.

Another pancake to try is the southern Indian dosa. They can be made with all sorts of grains, but the most common is made from rice and, usually, urad dahl. The grains are soaked, ground to a batter and fermented before being fried. They're hard to make at home. In Leicester we met **Dharmesh Lakhani** from the iconic Bobby's, a fixture on the city's Golden Mile for over 40 years. He brought dosas filled with spiced lentils, chutneys and pickles. Anna Jones got a bit nostalgic

remembering the table dosas – the size of the actual table – she had when she first encountered dosas.

Pancakes are incredibly versatile. Tim Anderson loves the Japanese version, okonomiyaki. *Okonomi* means 'as you like it', while *yaki* means 'cooked' – it is the ultimate personalised pancake.

Okonomiyaki

You want to start with a batter: 60ml water, 100g flour, 2 eggs, ¼ teaspoon baking powder, a big pinch each of salt and sugar and, if you have it, dashi powder. Finely chop 2 spring onions and ½ a hispi cabbage (do not use normal cabbage!). That's your base. (This amount should make 2 pancakes, but you can just make one massive one.) After this, it is all about the fillings. You really need 5 key ingredients to make this properly: okonomiyaki or okonomi sauce, which is sweet Japanese brown sauce (tonkatsu sauce will also work, at a pinch); Japanese mayonnaise; red pickled ginger; aonori (green seaweed flakes); and katsobushi (dried, smoked, tuna flakes). You can then add any other filling you fancy – prawns, kimchi, seeds etc. Just add them to your batter and fry it (Tim says you will probably need to add a lid to steam the pancakes too, making sure they are properly cooked through). You can also use pork belly, thinly cut like bacon, and briefly fried before the batter is poured on.

I'm after recipes for savoury pancakes suitable for vegetarians – no bacon allowed.

Hopefully you're now convinced that there is a lot of life beyond Pancake Day. But if you prefer to stick to a basic batter, and put your efforts into the toppings, what then? Rachel McCormack recommends cooking down spinach or rocket and adding raisins, pine nuts and sherry. Or you could try poached pears and Stilton. For a traditional British pancake, the secret is a filling that will stay inside, with an even texture so it doesn't tear the pancake when you roll it. But you can fudge the texture. Try blitzing an otherwise lumpy cauliflower cheese in a food processor to make it smoother – and oomph up the flavour with lots of mustard.

If you prefer more texture to your toppings, we're back to pancake forms you don't roll. Both American buttermilk pancakes and some northern European forms have raising agents in, whether it's bicarbonate of soda or yeast. They tend to be made into smaller, thicker, cakes than those you can roll and are sometimes stacked. Tim Anderson recommends a lumberjack stack – blueberry pancakes, smoky bacon, breakfast sausage and maple syrup. He says the salty-sweet contrast with the tartness of the blueberries is one of his favourite things.

And lastly, our audience at Chawton House, Hampshire, gave us a majority vote declaring that they remove the After Eight wrappers from the box after eating them (other after-dinner mints are, of course, available). But with around 30% opting to leave them in, it wasn't the whitewash some of the panellists bet on. Are you a neat freak, or do you like to add a little frisson of excitement to your everyday life? We won't judge: the panel was pretty split too.

POP
POP
POP
POP
NEWCASTLE
BROWN ALE

March

Dates for the calendar this month:

St David's Day (Leeks! Lamb! Bara brith!)

St Piran's Day (national day of Cornwall, break out the clotted cream and pasties)

Dalemain Mansion Marmalade Festival (includes a marmalade cat contest, who wouldn't want to go?)

British Pie Week (this needs no explanation)

Purim (Jewish Festival of Lots – time to eat hamantaschen, triangular filled sweet pastries)

St Patrick's Day (truly a month for Celtic culinary carnivals)

Holi (Hindu Festival of Spring: gujiya dumplings and, um, cannabis lassi)

The moon this month is made of **Parmesan**

Ubiquitous in Italian cuisine, the baby-sick-flavoured shavings on offer at supermarkets pale when compared to a properly aged wheel. Produced since the thirteenth century, it keeps well and was always expensive. Henry VIII got one for Christmas once. Pepys notoriously buried his to save it from the Great Fire of London.

This month *The Kitchen Cabinet* is in **Newcastle**, known for its contrasting architecture – industrial chic meets modern cool – and for stotties and pease pudding washed down with brown ale.

Key flavours for March are the first **asparagus**, **wild garlic**, **nettles**, **forced winter chicory** and the last of the **purple sprouting broccoli** – yes, spring is here.

And we are also pondering:

- How to stop things cooking when they reach perfection
- The best way to label food for the freezer
- What we love about the sounds of the kitchen
- How old is too old in the spice cupboard?
- And the best way to cook rice

Welcome to Newcastle upon Tyne, a city notorious for its nightlife, its unmistakable Geordie accent and whose irrepressible appetite for life is echoed in its food scene.

From its Roman roots to its role as a bulwark against Scottish invasion, Newcastle has long had a reputation for being tough to crack and ready for anything. Its shipbuilding and coal industries helped fuel the Industrial Revolution, and its 29 branches of Greggs (which was founded in the city) helped fuel our panel as they limbered up to tackle our audience questions. We've visited Newcastle twice, such is its culinary richness, memorably sitting down to half a pig's head for one of our post-show feasts.

Quick-fire question: *Should I throw out my elderly dried spices?*

Lots of you have contacted us both to ask about keeping old spices and to tell us tales of just how old some of them are. Rachel McCormack has a 10-year rule for her spice cupboard: older than that, and it's out. Prof. Barry Smith says most of the time that's fine. They will lose their flavour, and in some cases do so pretty quickly (Szechuan peppercorns are especially notorious for flaking out after a few months). But as long as they were well-sourced and of good quality, they shouldn't do you any harm. However, do be careful – those spice blends you bring back from the little market stall on holiday might be damp, and then bacteria can grow. Common sense most definitely applies.

Panellist pick: *Food sounds*

Whether it's the pop of a wine cork or the crunch of crisp crackling, we all have our favourite food sounds. Jay Rayner leapt in with his love for the soft, sucking plop that a spoon makes when plunged into a trifle (Dr Zoe Laughlin calls this a trifle fart). Rob Owen-Brown rhapsodises over the crunchy squelch of deshelling a boiled crab, while Sue Lawrence goes gooey for the plop-plop-plop of porridge in a pan (though she reserves the right to love the fut-fut-fut of a steaming suet pudding as well). Meanwhile, Anna Jones plumps for the pop of popping popcorn, the crack of mustard seeds as they meet the heat and, last but definitely not least, the sharp snap as her spoon breaks into a perfectly caramelised crème brûlée.

Stotties

Newcastle has more than its fair share of upmarket restaurants and Michelin-rated eating experiences. But supping on a sophisticated sourdough with a slate of whipped butter is but one end of the Geordie bread spectrum. We asked our audience to shout out the city's bread of choice and, without even the shadow of a prompt, back came the proud response: 'Stotty!'

So, what exactly is this yeasty delicacy? Found across North East England, it hasn't made it out of the area, despite the pleas of homesick natives on the Greggs website. We welcomed baker **Ian Thomson** to the show to induct us into its delights.

Brandishing a stotty in either hand, he explained that they were the plainest of breads, originally made either as a way of testing the oven before better loaves went in, or as a catch-all leftover loaf. They were based on a yeasted dough, but anything lying around was habitually added – pastry, biscuit dough, offcuts of other loaves – all mixed up, rolled roughly, proved very quickly and thrown in the oven. The result is a flattish loaf of an impressive diameter – Ian's were about 15cm across, with a light dimple pressed into the centre.

At its most basic, a stotty is a slow-baked bread. It's now also known as an oven-bottom bread, cooked on the base of the oven but, as Dr Annie Gray pointed out, prior to the introduction of cast-iron ovens in the nineteenth century, ovens didn't have shelves: in brick beehive ovens there is only the bottom. The word stotty has disputed origins. One meaning is 'to bounce or rebound' and Ian admitted that the older ones could be pretty dense. Something stotty-like has, however, always existed right across bread-baking cultures. A quickly made, cheap, leftover-based loaf, which was shoved in the oven to avoid waste, is a staple of both home cooks and commercial bakeries.

Obviously, the best stotties are filled with ham and pease pudding. But if I run out (as if) what else can I use to stuff my stotty?

Today, stotties are largely used as the basis for sandwiches. Our audience muttered slightly at the thought of fillings other than the Newcastle standard of ham and pease pudding, but we did have some brave souls who admitted that they added mustard ('controversially'), hummus and, in one case, salt and vinegar crisps and half an inch of salted butter. We also had a vote for using them to make superlative garlic bread.

Adding bacon is a TKC staple and, not to let Newcastle down, Rob Owen-Brown went one better, suggesting that a no-nonsense bread like a stotty needed an equally no-nonsense filling: crispy fried Spam, runny eggs and brown sauce. He was also keen on a pie barm, which, for those not familiar with Wigan and its gastronomic secrets, is a meat pie in a roll. Mince pie, of course, and Rob says if you want to supersize it, stick in some potato scallops as well. Or go potato scallops and a Manchester egg, a sort of Northern city food scarf sweep. If you're wondering quite how all of that will fit into a human mouth, it's simple. Just squash it down, and open (very) wide.

'If putting your leftovers in a stotty is wrong, I don't want to be right.' – Tim Anderson

If the thought of stuffing your stotty with the remains of other meals appeals, you aren't alone. Tim Anderson was adamant that anything would work in a stotty. He points to Japan, where breads filled with unusual savoury fillings are commonplace. Try a kare pan, which means 'curry bread'. He describes it as a sort of breadcrumbed doughnut filled with curry, a portable pouch of on-the-go goodness. You can make them with meat or vegetables. He is also keen on yaki soba pan, which is – you've guessed it – stir-fried noodles (yaki soba) stuffed, cold, into a hot dog bun. As carb-on-carb goes, it's a winner.

Sue Lawrence is a little more down to earth, pointing out that a stotty can be used for anything you might dream of in a simple sandwich. Sticking to the stotty's working-class roots, she likes to use allotment produce, such as roast beetroot. Adding goat's cheese, horseradish, dill and a positively Mediterranean touch of olive oil gives it all a modern twist.

You'll have noticed that we side-stepped the elephant in the room, the ham-pease pudding combo. But we could not go to Newcastle without both sampling it and talking about it. We just felt it needed exposing in all its glory, and not be confined to an (admittedly excellent) sandwich.

Top tip: ***How to stop your food continuing to cook towards the end of making a dish***

There's a reason so many chefs like to finish their sauces by *monter au beurre* – adding small cubes of well-chilled butter. Not only does it enhance the flavour and gloss but adding ice-cold butter also stops the sauce from cooking. Tim Hayward says the same trick can be used to stop your scrambled eggs from tipping over the edge or to cool easily ruined vegetables. Classically trained Sophie Wright plunges her vegetables into iced water (cold water with an ice cube in) for just a few seconds after boiling. It won't cool them down enough to make them unpleasant, but it will help keep the crunch. She says to make sure to remove them from the water immediately and dry them on kitchen towel. Reheat when needed in loads and loads of butter. It's the perfect way to get ahead of time when hosting a dinner party or cooking veg for a green bean salad or something similar.

Pease pudding

Is it a side dish? Is it a dip? Is it a spread? It's been called Geordie pâté (and hummus) and there's a pervading urban myth about the unwary southerner (usually a politician) pointing at it in a chip shop and requesting that nice guacamole. In Newcastle it is often used as a sandwich filling and you can buy it in tins. What is it?

Old is the answer, according to Annie Gray. Pease was originally both the singular and plural – but it sounded weird and so pea came into use for the lone vegetable. The word goes back to Old English, and dried peas were a staple back into antiquity. Green, grey, black, brown or yellow, they were soaked, cooked and eaten in a wide variety of forms. One of the most pervasive was as pease porridge, pottage or, later, pudding. All three names are interchangeable, depending on where in the country you are eating it. And then, of course, there are also mushy peas, not exactly a million miles removed, usually just a little bit less finely mushed.

Of course, you can eat it cold from the pot, but warming it up is quite a lot better.

The basic principle is the same for all: cooked peas, mashed down and seasoned. As with any apparently simple recipe though, people throughout history have put their own infinite spins on it. The Tudors added capers, the Stuarts opted for some onion, and black pudding works very well as well. On our Nottingham show, Annie brought the classic eighteenth-century version of pease pudding, which was a staple of the working classes. It's based on a type of one-pot cookery that went on in some areas until the 1950s.

Pease pudding

You want about a pint of split peas – it doesn't matter which type. Tie them fairly loosely into a muslin bag and then put them in to boil in a large pot of water. The real secret is to boil other things at the same time. Bacon was by far the most popular, so a ham hock or a piece of gammon is perfect, but you might also want to boil onions, carrots or even a potato too. Put them in another muslin bag and simmer the two together until the peas are soft – about an hour. Then take out your bag of peas and purée them. Add a bit of pepper – there's no need to salt because the ham will have seasoned them for you. Add a couple of eggs, mix well, and then wet and flour a pudding cloth (or grease a basin). Throw in the mixture, tie it up tight, and boil it for another hour or so. Serve the pudding in chunks, accompanied by a small piece of ham or bacon, plus the vegetables. You can serve the boiling liquid as a broth on the side.

Rob Owen-Brown devoured this with gusto, commenting that it just needed frying in lard to be perfect. Rob makes his pease pudding by boiling split peas with ham hock, which he then adds into the pea purée when he mashes it. He also adds garam masala. But like most modern cooks (and many historic ones), he leaves out the eggs and doesn't make it into a solid pudding. Until, that is, the next day, when he adds flour and makes it into pease pudding fritters. Fried, of course, in bacon fat.

'We all love peas, don't we? All those fairs and markets across the North of England: black peas, little pot, vinegar on top, beautiful.'
– Rob Owen-Brown

The fifth Sunday in Lent brings with it Carlin Sunday, named for a type of dried pea. Also known as pigeon peas, black peas, grey peas and the evocative black badgers, carlin peas are eaten whole, rather than mushy, as a street food in the North West. Plain boiled, they are generally served with salt and pepper, plus vinegar, which adds a much-needed acidity to the natural sweetness of the peas.

Tim Hayward agrees that vinegar is vital to any dried puréed pea mix. He serves mushy peas as part of his Christmas lunch, making sure he has way more than he needs. Collected together and squished down with the leftover potatoes the next day, he fries them in bacon grease and serves them as a sort of mushy pea frittata, heaped with pickles and offcuts from the joint.

You can use any dried pea for mushy peas or pease pudding. Sophie Wright favours marrowfat peas, soaked overnight with a pinch of bicarbonate of soda to help soften them. She adds a pinch of sugar when she boils them and says they are an intrinsic part of any fish and chip supper.

I recently bought a load of split peas in an attempt to eat more pulses. But apart from pease pudding, I don't actually know what to do with them. Any ideas?

On one of our visits to Liverpool we met chef **Dave Critchley**, a man intent upon resurrecting the traditional foodways of the city. He uses split peas – and lentils – to make peawack. It's a riff on the theme of one-pot cookery, and formerly eaten by the working classes of the city. He makes it by boiling a ham and peas and saving the stewing water. The ham is used for one meal, while the peas go back into the stock with any ham offcuts and whatever vegetables, cooked or raw, you have lying around. It's the ultimate in economy soups. Best served with a hunk of bread and a mug of beer.

Top tip: ***Foolproof food labelling for the fridge and freezer***

We've all had the issue where we go to defrost what we think are chicken breasts, but they turn out to be pigs' bladders (or that may just be Annie Gray). But what's the solution? Whiteboard markers rub off, sticky labels fall off, permanent markers fade, label makers rely on single-use plastics, and after 20 uses it's hard to find a space on the box for any of them. Help is at hand though. Annie says she was embroiled in a brilliant thread of household hacks on Twitter, out of which came the answer: microporous tape. It sticks, it stays, you can write on it in biro as well as marker pen, and it is (generally) biodegradable.

Cooking with beer

Now we've mentioned beer, we obviously have to mention it a bit more. The biggest-selling bottled beer of the 1970s to the early 1990s, and a pure Proustian hit for anyone who was a student in those decades, is Newcastle Brown Ale. Most of us know it as Newkie Brown, Broon or, apparently, 'dog', as in 'I'm going to see a man about a ...' When he was a student in Los Angeles, Tim Anderson says it was never shortened, for in comparison to the other ales on offer, this was the really good stuff.

'We'd call it by its proper name. You'd order a Newcastle Brown Ale and the bartender would know you were a man of the world.' – Tim Anderson

Newkie Brown is brewed specifically as a bottled beer. The five points on the blue star on its logo represent the five breweries that came together to form Newcastle Breweries, the company behind its invention in 1927 (it is now made in the Netherlands by Heineken). Brown ales were the height of fashion at this time, part of a wider trend toward nostalgic tastes, which included milds.

Rob Owen-Brown isn't a fan but says you can use it as the basis for a cream dessert. Just mix Newkie Brown – or any other mild or brown ale – with double cream, condensed milk, honey, cinnamon and nutmeg.

If that sounds like a weird beer custard, rest assured it isn't that far off a recipe with a much longer heritage.

Annie Gray says it sounds like beer caudle, which was a sort of egg-thickened beer custard, often used medicinally and pimped with warming spices such as ginger. It evolved in turn into beer soup, a hugely popular dish in eighteenth-century Germany, and taken to America by German settlers there. Annie favours the earlier versions but has never quite plucked up the courage to try one recipe in her armoury, which involves a pint each of beer and port, plus cinnamon, cloves and sugar. It's served with bread croutons, which seems like overkill, frankly.

I'm keen to be adventurous at cooking with beer, but I get stuck at steak and ale pie. Is there anything quick and easy I could try?

Jordan Bourke also recommends blending beer with sweetened cream or, even better, custard. But don't stop there, make it into ice cream. It's worth experimenting with the beer you use. Stout is a classic, especially milk stout, but any sweetish beer will work. Try a chocolate stout, a flavoured porter or one of the sweeter classic real ales. If you favour heavy hopping, have a go with those too.

If you aren't convinced by making ice cream, you could always stick to the halfway house. Tim Anderson likes a beer float, which is just beer in a glass with a complementary flavour of ice cream. A chocolate stout with a good dollop of salted caramel ice cream would work, but you could also try mild with hazelnut ice cream or imperial stout with coffee ice cream.

What about savoury options? Back to Tim, who says all those German settlers with their beer soups had quite an influence on Wisconsin cuisine. However, if you mix beer soup with what's basically the state dish of Wisconsin – cheese – you get a modern beer soup, which is all-American (but tastes quite a lot like liquid Welsh rarebit).

Beer soup, the Wisconsin Way

Tim uses a dark German lager with a bit of smoked malt, mixed with smoked Italian cheese (provolone) and a lot of Red Leicester. Add a little bit of onion, celery and some thyme and then your liquid, which should be half beer, half stock.

Nisha Katona says beer makes a brilliant batter. Use gram (chickpea) flour mixed with beer – an IPA works well – with some nigella seeds thrown in. Then just dip in whatever vegetables you want to use: try onions, broccoli and green beans for starters. Deep-fry them and serve with the beer you used for the batter.

Zoe Laughlin agrees. She adds that alcohol boils at a lower temperature than water, around 80°C. This means that a mixture with beer in will therefore dry out and crisp up quicker. Plus, the bubbles add a lightness.

If you aren't as keen as the TKC panel on deep-frying, you could still use it for batter – how about a pancake? A savoury topping such as cheese or cauliflower cheese would be ideal. You could even make the cheese sauce with beer instead of milk.

Depending on the beer, you can swap it in for other things. In the Burton-on-Trent show we talked to beer writer Pete Brown, who said you could use beer for most of the things you'd use wine for. His go-to is coq à la bière, a twist on coq au vin. Of you can use it for moules marinières.

Sophie Wright says beer is also a good tenderiser. Heard of Rocky Mountain oysters? They are bull's testicles, battered and fried. Sophie recommends tenderising them by peeling and slicing the testicles and soaking the slices in beer for 6 hours. Then dust them in flour, cayenne pepper and fry them in butter. You can't get better balls.

Be careful when cooking with really hoppy beers. If you boil them too much, you'll release the wrong flavours and just get nasty, acrid, bitterness.

Be careful what beer you choose, says Tim Anderson. You can't go wrong with German lagers but be very careful with bitters and anything too hoppy. He is fond of bratwurst boiled in beer but tells the cautionary tale of the time he boiled them in a modern American IPA, whose strong hoppiness had a whiff of mango about it. Result? Mango-flavoured bratwurst. Not exactly the desired result.

These are all nice, light options, but it's March and still chilly out. What about something to warm us up while we wait for spring to properly arrive? Andi Oliver makes a dark stout gravy for her burgers – she uses Guinness, but any dry stout will work.

Beef burgers with stout gravy

You want to start with an oxtail and braise that slowly with beef stock, stout, treacle, cinnamon, nutmeg, black cardamom, red chillies and star anise – all the dark spices. It'll need 5–6 hours to get really, really soft. Take out the oxtail and reduce the cooking liquid right down to make an amazing gravy. Use the oxtail in your burgers: strip the meat off and mix that with a bit of minced chuck (braising steak), plus enough breadcrumbs and egg to just bind it together – not too much or it'll go pappy. Make it into patties, fry them off until they are nice and brown, and then put them in the oven. Serve the burgers in a bun with the sauce on the side in a little pot, so you can pour it, but then also use your bun to get right in the corners. Or your fingers. Fingers work too.

IPA soda bread

If you want to take it to the next level, you could always serve your burgers with stout gravy and beer bread. Jordan Bourke makes a soda bread using IPA. Just add a teaspoon each of bicarbonate of soda and baking powder, around 300ml beer, 200ml water and a tablespoon of blackstrap molasses to 500g flour and a good teaspoon of salt. Mix it all up lightly, put it into a greased tin and bake for 45 minutes at 180°C. Remove from the tin, and put it back in the oven for another 5–10 minutes to firm up the sides and bottom.

Asparagus

Before you rush off to the kitchen to start slicing your scrotums and braising in beer, hang on just a moment. This is all rather brown and beige. But as spring creeps in upon us, the first fronds of green are appearing in our gardens and in our greengrocers. It's nearly the season for one of the most eagerly awaited vegetables around and one which, in our view, is definitely worth waiting for. It doesn't travel well, it has a short but stimulating season, and it has one of the most brilliant alternative names around. We're talking, of course, about asparagus or, as some of us like to whisper to ourselves when feeling down, sparrowgrass. You see? Who wouldn't fall in love with such a fabulously named foodstuff?

Last month's foray into all things lusty gave us the surprising fact that 7% of you reckon asparagus was the thing that does it for you. But Annie Gray says that amazingly, despite their phallic appearance, **they were a rare thing not regarded as an aphrodisiac in the past.** Although the Romans cultivated and ate it, we didn't start growing it seriously in Britain until the sixteenth century. It was pretty puny stuff, with thin stalks (hence, presumably, the grass bit of sparrowgrass). It was only after intense breeding and a real asparagus craze in the next few centuries that the thick, fleshy shafts we know and love today appeared. By the nineteenth century, some spears were eye-wateringly huge.

I've never been adventurous with my vegetables. I love the idea of asparagus, but I tend to just steam it. What else can I do?

Let's start with the classics: there's a reason steamed or boiled asparagus with hollandaise sauce is the thing everybody thinks of. It works.

Andi Oliver says don't feel it's wrong to do obvious stuff, but you could try and embrace the tempuras and fritters. Or try chargrilling – just get a really, really hot pan and roast them off with a little bit of salt. She serves the asparagus with a curly parsley aioli – just blitz mayonnaise with parsley and garlic and use it as a dip. Maybe a parsley scone on the side … Another of Andi's seasonal recipes, something to truly showcase the asparagus, is a simple fricassee.

Asparagus fricassee

Char the asparagus, set it aside and then grab some nice peas, some fresh spring greens, all the lovely, bright spring vegetables. Sauté these in a little bit of butter, then finish with lemon juice and a bit of vegetable stock. Simmer very briefly just to cook it all through and serve with a lovely piece of charred fish, plus your asparagus, added back at the last minute. It's a really beautiful, vibrant, bang-on seasonal way to eat something like that.

Paula McIntyre agrees that certain flavours just work. Black pudding is a popular accompaniment, but she prefers to use guanciale – pork-cheek bacon cured with garlic and other herbs. The best bit is the level of fat. She renders it down, taking out the bacon when it is crisped and leaving the fat. Stick your asparagus in the fat and cook it gently. Then she adds lemon zest and juice and fennel, plus loads of parsley and serves it with the crispy guanciale bacon on top.

Umami-rich flavours are key, says Tim Anderson, who does a Japanese dish called asparabacon. You've probably guessed the essence already, but it's not just spears wrapped in bacon, but spears chopped into pieces and wrapped in bacon. Thread them onto skewers and grill them. Tim Hayward uses cheese to add umami to his asparagus. He just rubs the spears in olive oil, puts them on a baking tray and layers Parmesan on top. Bake until crisp and just starting to scorch.

'My daughter eats them like chips, and I can't argue.' – Tim Hayward

You could, of course, combine both the Tims' recipes together and wrap your spears in bacon – Parma ham or similar is even better – lay them on a baking sheet and top them with Parmesan. Grill or bake until you can't wait any more. Serve as is, or with a poached egg. You could even go for a boiled egg and use your hammy, cheesy, sparrowgrass spears as soldiers.

If you've already eaten all the bacon, Jordan Bourke is here to save the day. He warns that it is easy to overcook asparagus. Why not try it raw? He shaves the spears

You'll need to make notes when you try the recipes, so here's a handy gap.

lengthways with a vegetable peeler to get thin strips, which naturally curl. Put them into a salad bowl and add in some lemon zest and really good olive oil. You can add other vegetables too – the shaved fennel that Paula likes, whatever herbs you fancy. Toss it all up, sit back and feast.

The best way to cook basmati rice:
To soak or not to soak, that is the question

Jordan Bourke is a soaker. He rinses the rice until the water runs clear, puts it in a pan with twice the quantity of water, brings it to the boil and simmers for 10–12 minutes. Then he puts the lid on and leaves it to soak up any residual water.

Nah, says **Andi Oliver**, a cursory rinse is fine, it's all about the flavour. Garlic, onions and spices, all fried up, then get the rice in and really coat it. She recommends getting cinnamon in there, and black cardamom for a smoky flavour. And for really next level basmati, use stock, not water – 20 minutes at a very low heat. Or, let's face it, in a rice cooker.

And lastly, for this month's audience member in the spotlight ... we wondered, what was the oldest item in your freezer?

We asked this question on our show in the Royal Botanic Gardens, Kew. One audience member had a packet of frozen peas so old she couldn't recall buying them, but said they were still useful, having been applied to her son's broken nose, husband's dodgy elbow and myriad injuries in between. Going one better was the cocktail lover who said they didn't really know what was at the bottom of their freezer as it was so caked in ice. But the ice was the point – ideal, apparently, for espresso martinis.

The TKC call sheet

The Kitchen Cabinet action happens over one fun-filled hour, in live shows recorded at locations across the UK. You can get tickets to attend through the BBC Shows and Tours page.

However, like the proverbial swan, sliding gracefully across a still pond with its legs going like crazy underneath, it takes a lot of planning to get *The Kitchen Cabinet* on the road.

1 week before: The venue is booked, the panel selected, and the production assistants are busy checking for unexpected train strikes. The show's producer gets to work contacting panellists, sending ideas for themes and requesting initial thoughts, including expressions of true horror. Concurrently, the search starts for local food heroes with stories to tell.

4 days before: Phone calls with panellists. A lengthy process as all love to talk. The show starts to take shape.

3 days before: Back and forth with panellists, producer and Jay to create an outline script.

5 hours before: Panellists and Jay start their journeys to the venue.

4 hours before: Someone sets up a WhatsApp group. Panellists work out whether they are on the same train. Someone claims they have a deadline and can everyone go away. Someone else picked up the wrong tickets and needs to meet urgently to swap them over with whoever has theirs.

3½ hours before: Panic over; panellists are convening in small groups on the train and catching up. Jay tells us to save food talk for the show. Whoever is driving is stuck in a traffic queue.

3–4 hours before: Call time for the production team at the venue. They set up tables to welcome our audience, check fire regs, sort out a green room, unpack snacks, work out stage seating, and text any last-minute instructions to the increasingly excited panellists, who by now have set aside any pretence at work and are swapping restaurant recommendations.

3 hours before: Call time for the sound team. They hook up the broadcast van to the power and start setting up microphones.

2 hours before: Call time for the panellists and Jay, who arrive in a cab driven by someone a little wild about the eyes after 20 minutes in a small space with five people yelling about food, laden with plastic boxes full of food and wondering what the food will be like on the show.

105 minutes before: Sound check, during which some calm is restored by the serenity of the sound team. Usually we tell everyone what we had for breakfast to test sound levels. Sometimes we make it up. Peacock pie always sounds better than tepid toast and dubious butter. Jay gives a pep talk that boils down to not being terrible.

90 minutes before: The production assistant goes on a coffee run. There's a secret Nespresso machine in the broadcast van. It's been known for panellists to sneak off and beg pitifully for a caffeine fix. The audience is arriving now (sometimes they've been queuing for hours) and are filling in their pop quizzes and audience question sheets. Our local food hero has arrived. If they've brought food, the panellists have to be physically restrained from falling on it.

1 hour before: Jay secretes himself in a tiny room full of question sheets and starts to go through them with the producer. He takes regular breaks to come and raid the rapidly dwindling crisp and pork scratchings pile provided in the green room. The producer goes through the outline script with the panellists.

15 minutes before: Jay reveals the questions, and the panellists go to battle with each other over who gets the easy answers and who is going to say what. He reminds everyone to have a wee now or never and leaves to go on stage.

10 minutes before: The panellists are gathered, the producer reminds the audience that the show airs at 10.30am and 3.00pm and might be listened to as a podcast, so please don't say good evening. Jay sweeps onto stage to rapturous applause.

5 minutes before: Panellists announced, run in to more applause, and there is then an anticlimactic pause while we all shift in our seats, put out food, move water around, shuffle papers and …

0 minutes: The show begins.

SOUP
BARBARA
CARTLAND

April

Significant food events this month:

The start of Ramadan (the Muslim Holy Month, a month of fasting during daylight hours, culminating in Eid al-Fitr – the Festival of Fast Breaking. Foods vary: try dates, baklava and honey cake for starters)

Carlin Sunday (peas, glorious peas)

London Coffee Festival (latte art, but also cocktails. Presumably nobody sleeps for a while afterwards)

York Chocolate Festival (chocolate sculptures, trails and eating)

Passover (matzah, roast eggs and bitter herbs, among other things, all hugely symbolic on the Seder plate)

Easter (where to start? Good Friday for fish, Easter Sunday for the end of Lent and the return of meat. Plus, eggs of all kinds, including the French town of Haux's giant omelette: 5218 eggs anyone?)

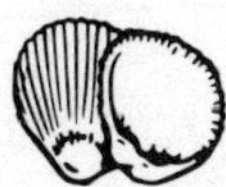

Bakewell Food Festival

The moon this month is made of **Cerney Ash**

A goat's cheese from Gloucestershire, this shares its seasonality with its French model, Valençay. It's an unpasteurised soft goat's cheese, tangy and fresh. Available, like any fresh soft cheese, only when the goats are lactating, it's a good cheese to start with for those who aren't sure they will like a full-on goaty tang.

This month *The Kitchen Cabinet* is in **Swansea**, known for things salty and sea-flavoured, from seaweed to cockles, and bracing windswept rambles around the Gower Peninsula.

Key flavours this month include **new-season lamb**, **radishes**, **rocket** and the last **shellfish** until the autumn.

And we are also thinking about:

- How to add sparkle to your store-cupboard staples
- The best way to make a bacon sandwich
- Recommendations for retro food books
- Whether to wash mushrooms
- And your most alarming restaurant experiences

Welcome to Swansea, Wales's second city and a bustling hub for surfers, swimmers and other beach bods, all seeking sustenance after a long day on the sands.

Once nicknamed Copperopolis, Swansea was the centre of the copper smelting industry in the UK, providing pots and pans to a nation of cooks. The copper is mainly gone now, unless you count the light of the evening sun catching the waves on Swansea Bay. We thought about walking from the Marina to Mumbles, just because the neighbouring Victorian honeypot village has such a great name, but we got sidetracked by our venue at the National Waterfront Museum.

We also got distracted by the onset of Easter. Gambolling lambs in the surrounding salt marshes, fluffy bunnies fleeing the train we came in on, and the Manchester eggs Rob Owen-Brown brought with him for the journey. Yes, all the goodness of Easter is here, and we want to help you turn it into dinner.

Top tip: ***Bored of baked beans? This tip will have you back in love***

Jordan Bourke says there's an easy way to boost your beans. Just add butter. Salted butter. Stir in a tablespoon when heating. The richness of the butter tempers the acidity of the beans for instant, never-go-back velvetiness.

Salt marsh lamb

A leg of lamb has long been part of the Easter feast. It has links to the Jewish Passover, a holiday marking the exodus of the Jews from Egypt. According to the biblical book of Exodus, God visited 10 plagues upon the Egyptians to persuade them to free the Israelites. One of them was the death of every first-born son – except in those houses marked as being Jewish by being anointed with lamb's blood. A lamb bone remains part of the Orthodox Seder feast, held the evening before the start of Passover, and it's from this root that notions of the sacrificial lamb or the lamb of God later sprang.

It helps, of course, that lamb comes into season around Easter. For a long time, Britain bred sheep predominantly for their wool, making lamb a rarity, and prestige always helps push a meat into the realms of celebratory food. That meant Christmas – lambs reared in barns for the Christmas market were called house lamb – and Easter. Grass lamb was the name given to just-weaned lambs, which remained expensive until the very end of the nineteenth century. It wasn't until New Zealand started exporting its surplus lambs that it came down in price.

West of Swansea on the Gower Peninsula, you'll find a specific type of lamb that is well worth seeking out. Salt marsh lamb is, as the name suggests, bred and raised on the salty marshland of the Burry estuary. On our Swansea show was **Will Pritchard** from Gower Salt Marsh Lamb. His family have been farming on the Gower since the 1960s.

'We can get quite precious and cheffy about food, but I think salt marsh lamb is one of those things that's real, and worth paying the extra for.'
– Rob Owen-Brown

Will's sheep graze on tidal marshland. The vegetation they feast on is utterly different to the plants more sheltered sheep eat. His graze on samphire and marsh grasses, sorrel and sea lavender, all of which get washed by the tide twice a day. At spring tides (the highest high tides), the sheep come off the marsh – brought in with a mixture of Land Rover horns and sheepdogs – but otherwise their diet is almost all that of the unique environment of the estuary. Sheep are what they eat just as much as any other animal, and it all means that the flavour and texture of the meat are distinctive and different.

Tim Hayward is cynical. He points out that the salinity of meat is governed by that of the body, and you don't get saltier meat just because an animal eats saltier things. But the flavour of salt marsh lamb isn't really about the salt. The meat is leaner, darker, sweeter and slightly stronger than conventional lamb, not saltier. That's just the public perception.

Rob Owen-Brown is a huge fan. He says it is even better as hogget, which is essentially a teenage sheep, older than lamb but not yet adult enough to be mutton.

But what about cooking with salt marsh lamb? Will says you can do anything you would with any other piece of lamb, but given its premium price, it makes sense to prepare it plainly. He advises using methods that will let the flavours soar. Grilled chops, plain roasts or lightly seasoned lamb meatballs.

I love the idea of lamb but I'm a bit scared of cooking it. What can I make for my Easter feast which will wow people, but not be really difficult?

Andi Oliver starts with one fundamental piece of advice: please season your meat. It isn't scary and it makes all the difference. She urges you to get in and handle your meat. Get to know the joint and know your own tastes.

If you are scared of over-salting, try a rub. Her go-to is just allspice, cumin and orange zest, plus shredded bay leaves, thyme, flat-leaf parsley, garlic and either some chilli or cayenne. She says for best results, get it inside the meat, not just on the surface, so punch holes in your joint with a skewer and mix the spice blend with oil – 50:50 works well. Stick the joint in a large bowl (or the sink), rub it all over and leave it for 20 minutes before you roast it. Don't forget that you've already salted it – so taste it when you are carving before you start adding any more. If you want to go even more basic, try some coarsely ground toasted coriander seeds, mixed with a good pinch of salt. Just rub it all over and roast as normal.

Beer-brined roast lamb

You can also brine it. Paula McIntyre suggests 500ml each of pale ale and water, 125g sea salt and 75g of sugar or sugar and honey. Leave overnight, drain, roast – and then boil up some more of your beer with a little bit of honey to make a simple glaze to brush over towards the end of cooking. Timings, of course, depend on how well done you like your meat.

Roasting is the prestige way to prepare meat and has been for centuries. Nothing says feast like a glistening joint. Rachel McCormack favours stuffing a lamb leg with Mediterranean flavours: garlic and rosemary. It's done in Spain with a soft, largely milk-fed type of lamb called Ternasco de Aragón.

Garlic and rosemary wine-marinated lamb

Make small slits all over your lamb leg. Stuff these with sliced garlic and small sprigs of rosemary and marinate it all overnight in red wine. The next day, just pat it dry and roast it on a bed of potatoes. If you want to make it even easier, leave it in the wine, making sure it is well covered, and wrap the tin tightly in foil. Bake gently until the meat is falling off the bone. Celebrate the lamb, as well as the holiday.

Tim Hayward also likes using leg. He suggests raan, a Persian dish based on yoghurt and warm spices, such as coriander, cinnamon and cumin, plus ginger and garlic. You just smother the lamb in spicy yoghurt, leave it to marinate, and then roast it very slowly with a little water in the base of the tin. The tang of the yoghurt cuts through the fattiness of the lamb, and it's as good cold as it is hot.

Lamb can be fatty. Try pairing your roast meat with a sauce that will work with the flavour of lamb fat, rather than trying to hide it. Mint's the big one. In the seventeenth century, it was recommended as an excellent aid to digestion, made into a sauce with vinegar. But it may be too obvious. Angela Hartnett favours fruit – a gooseberry sauce made simply with gooseberries, a little sugar and some butter, all stewed down and seasoned, or something with sour plum. Andi Oliver opts for slowly caramelised onions, which she sweats down with garlic and fresh chillies, and then adds tamarind, dried chipotle chillies, red wine and brown sugar. She says it also makes a great BBQ sauce, if you fancy doing Easter outside.

Of course, if you really want to push the boat out, why stop at a leg? Rob Owen-Brown says if you happen to have a wood-fired outdoor oven handy, a 15–20kg whole lamb only takes around 6 hours to roast, and it is guaranteed to stop the show.

If you find that just a little bit baarmy (sorry), then how about something to go on the side? Something green and gooey, salty and, arguably, a tiny bit slimy. But incredibly good for you. Let's take a closer look at laverbread.

Quick-fire question: ***Should I wash my mushrooms?***

Rachel McCormack says life's too short. Cultivated mushrooms are pretty clean anyway and, especially if you are cooking them, they will be perfectly safe. You do need to get rid of the grit, but you can do that with a wipe and not a wash. Tim Anderson agrees, though he says it depends on the age of the fungi. Older ones may need peeling if they are getting slimy. Otherwise, just remove the dirt and you're good to go.

Laverbread

So, what is laverbread? Well, 16% of our audience in Neath, just a few miles up the road, agreed with the statement 'Nice to eat but looks like a cowpat'. The rest opted for the more diplomatic description of it as 'Welsh caviar'. It's made by boiling seaweed for – well – a long time and then mincing it to form a blackish-green, shiny purée. It's naturally salty and umami-rich, and nearly always bought ready-prepared.

In the audience in Neath was chef **Angela Gray**, who explained that laverbread was incredibly important in South Wales in particular, for it was a vital part of the diet of the local mining communities. Laverbread is high in a wide range of vitamins, along with other important dietary elements, and contains a lot of protein. Unlike many foods favoured by manual labourers in the past, who needed a lot of energy to get through their days, it is also low in calories. That, plus its distinctive taste and strong regional connection, has helped it remain popular today.

I know seaweed is really good for me, but I've only ever had it as crispy seaweed at my local Chinese. What can I do to get into it?

Traditional recipes for using laverbread are plain, but that doesn't mean they don't have tremendous TKC panel appeal. Laverbread was often mixed with oatmeal, then fried up with oats and eaten with cockles. It is even better with fried bacon added as well.

Rob Owen-Brown goes one better. He would like you to try it with oysters – just shuck them, spoon some laverbread on top, and crumble a bit of blue cheese on top of that. Grill for a few minutes, just to brown the cheese and make it bubbly, and serve. You can do the same with green-lipped mussels.

'It'll knock spots of a Rockefeller oyster any day.' – Rob Owen-Brown

Rob also likes laverbread – and seaweed more generally – dropped into pasta or risotto. It adds texture to a fish risotto, as well as adding colour contrast. It's also good added to warming Thai soups such as Tom Yum, a hot-and-sour soup, which is usually made with prawns.

In Scotland, laverbread is known as slook, says Rachel McCormack. She says that in Lewis, in the Western Isles, they add butter to the mix when boiling. Though, apparently, they also have a saying around boiling stones in butter so you may sup the brew – there is nothing they don't add butter to.

One of our audience members said they like to make posh canapés with laverbread. We very much liked the idea of turning basic workers' sustenance into haute cuisine with a Welsh crostini. Try good white bread, laverbread, a slice of bacon and a cockle, all very artfully presented. Or swap the bacon for date purée and the cockle for a few sprigs of samphire.

Seaweed is consumed widely beyond laverbread. Rachel says dried seaweeds are great as a vegan substitute for things like anchovies, to really add punch and umami to a stew or soup. Some fishmongers have also started selling fresh seaweed, which, depending on the variety, can be eaten raw or cooked. Most are excellent deep-fried (though, conversely, the deep-fried seaweed you ate in that Chinese restaurant was almost certainly just finely chopped kale). But check with your fishmonger when you buy it – some need cooking for several hours. Rachel recommends seaweed shortbread but says it's really good in dumplings or bread as well.

Most of the seaweed you'll see in mainstream shops will be Japanese, including nori, kombu and wakame. Tim Anderson uses all of them but says you can take them well beyond the uses they are often sold for. He uses nori as a sprinkle, but also makes seaweed butter and mayonnaise. Andi Oliver, meanwhile, uses wakame to enliven salad. Just soak to soften, chop it up and use it like spinach. She likes to mix it with some raw tuna, chopped avocado and a dressing of rice vinegar, sesame oil, minced ginger and toasted sesame seeds.

There's a really exciting science to all of this too. Prof. Peter Barham has worked with seaweeds on a molecular level. They contain polysaccharides, chains of sugar molecules, which can be extracted and used to make gels called alginates. Alginates have been used since the 1940s to make artificial cocktail cherries, using a gel with cherry flavour in, extruded through a tube into a bucket containing calcium salt and calcium ions. Coloured red, they taste of cherries, look like cherries but are much cheaper than cherries.

More recently, seaweed gels have been adopted enthusiastically by chefs such as Ferran and Albert Adrià at El Bulli and Heston Blumenthal of The Fat Duck. The artificial cherry idea inspired what's now known as spherification, which produces little balls of semi-liquid gel that look like fish roe. Seaweed gels can also be used to create a gel that turns to liquid in the mouth. A coffee jelly that you eat and then becomes a drink is a real showstopper at the end of a long meal. Peter cautions, though, if you do it the other way round – a coffee that then gels when it hits your tongue – it is less showstopper than dinner stopper. 'Disgusting' was his verdict.

Top tip: *How to better your brown sauce*

When Tim Hayward casually mentioned his version of a brown sauce as a substitute for gravy at the end of one of our lockdown shows, we were inundated with requests for the full recipe. Clearly, this was the content the nation needed, so banana bread begone. It's really simple. Just mix 3 parts brown sauce with 1 part sriracha (so, 75ml brown sauce, 25ml sriracha). Tim says it'll make your sausages sing arias and your mash a marvel. People have told him it has changed their life.

Panellist pick: *Retro cookbooks*

Rachel McCormack: *The Romance of Food* by Barbara Cartland every time. Embrace the pink, the frills and the surprisingly serious advice on food and love.

Tim Anderson: *The Anderson Family Cookbook*, because every family should have a collection of recipes, spiral-bound, and updated every decade (ish). It's retro, and modern, and a family history, all in one.

Tim Hayward: *Len Deighton's Action Cook Book*. Deighton is known for his thrillers, but he was also the food editor of the *Observer* and his book is not only excellent, but all executed as strip cartoons. Tim first saw it when he was 15, and the cover is a man with a shoulder holster making spaghetti with a woman in a negligée draped over him. Who wouldn't want to cook like that?

Dr Annie Gray: Fanny Cradock's cookery show tie-in pamphlets, which are a riot of colour and silliness in the gloom of post-war UK. Special mention for her 1970s 'Small Fry' pamphlet, in which she promotes a 'banana candle'. It isn't quite as lurid (well, phallic) as the 1920s candle salad Annie made for us in Pangbourne, but it isn't far off. Plus, it's rolled in nuts, and has texture.

Simnel cake and hot cross buns

Time now for something sweet after all that savoury saltiness. With Lent over, and eggs and dairy back on the menu, Easter is a time when many historically Christian cultures like to celebrate with a big, rich bun. In Russia you'll find kulich, while in Finland it's pääsiäisleipä. Then there's the dove-shaped Italian colomba and the German Osterklaben. All are based on yeasted doughs, enriched with spice and packed with dried fruit and nuts for good measure. The two most well-known British Easter bakes fall into exactly the same category. It's time to heat up our cross buns and slice our simnel cake.

Simnel cake is one of the most mythologised foods on the British calendar. If you hang about on the web you'll read that it was invented by a couple called Simon and Nelly after they had an argument that led to combining their baking desires. You'll also be told that it traditionally has 11 (or 12 or 13) balls on top, and that it was baked by female servants to take home to their mothers on Mothering Sunday. But Annie Gray says it's all rubbish.

Simple logic demolishes some parts of the simnel story. The name comes from a type of flour (simla) used by the Romans, and 'simnels' appear as a name for cakes in medieval bread regulations. The Simon–Nelly story started circulating in the eighteenth century, when the cake was sometimes boiled and then baked. By the nineteenth century it was strongly regional. The Bury version was yeast-raised and had a layer of almond paste in the middle; the Shrewsbury one was covered in pastry, egg-glazed and was (apparently) easily mistaken for a footstool.

'We owe most of our ideas about simnels to the 1930s. We sort of codify cake. I'm not sure it's a good thing'. – Annie Gray

Then there are the balls. They make a brief appearance in the Edwardian era, based on earlier designs, which have crenulations and look like a big pointy cushion. Most twentieth-century simnels involved walls of marzipan and icing, and luridly coloured ornaments of eggs, chickens and other Easter motifs. Some 1970s simnels have balls and chickens. The idea that the balls represent the apostles was a cute story invented after the fact.

The Mother's Day connection is also modern. Simnels were Easter cakes, only gradually gaining a Mothering Sunday connection. Mothering Sunday was originally a day when people went off to visit their 'mother' church, before it got subsumed by the American version of Mother's Day in the late nineteenth century. Servants sometimes got to march off to church – but the day wasn't associated with mothers, and since many servants worked hundreds of miles from their parents' homes, that all falls apart for periods prior to the early twentieth century too.

Still, it's a nice cake.

After unleashing the Annie Gray mythbuster, we hardly dared get on to hot cross buns, but apparently they are less controversial. They probably date to the Tudor era and, by the eighteenth century, they were a popular street food. Then they were only hot cross buns if they were, in fact, hot. As cross buns they were sold around Easter, hugely sought-after for breakfast, and hawked at elegant windows by bakers' boys bearing trays of hot buns on their heads.

Jordan Bourke says they are easy to make at home, and a great way to get into baking. He makes them with his toddler. He starts with an enriched yeasted dough – bread flour, milk, butter, salt, sugar, yeast and egg – and once he's kneaded it to the point where it is elastic, lets the dough really have it as he incorporates the dried fruit.

'I just let him take out all his three-year-old aggression on the hot cross buns.' – Jordan Bourke

It's a quickly risen dough, so ideal for showing children (or adults) with a low boredom threshold the results of their work fast. Key things to remember are to keep the dough moist – a dry bun is a disappointing bun – and to cook them quickly to avoid them drying out.

When it comes to cutting the cross, or putting it on with a separate paste, line them all up and do them at once, in a continuous line across and down. It's much quicker than trying to do each bun individually.

If you don't happen to have a child handy, you can knead in a stand mixer. Dr Zoe Laughlin points out that you can also go down the no-knead route. For a basic no-knead bread, all you have to do is mix the four basic ingredients together – flour, water, salt and yeast – and leave them overnight. To some extent, they will develop gluten and come together as the yeast ferments. The same technique can be applied to hot cross buns – mix all of the ingredients together and leave them overnight.

For a really good dough, kneading is important, and no-knead breads or buns won't be as fluffy. Kneading elongates and develops the gluten strands necessary for texture. It's also why many bread or yeasted bun recipes use strong flour, which has more protein in it. These proteins form the gluten strands, which are essentially an elastic network in your dough. When baked, they act like little elastic balloons, fluffing up, to give you the airy, light but slightly chewy structure you find in the best breads.

What's best – fresh or dried yeast?

It's getting easier to find fresh yeast in the UK now, but is it always the best option?

As long as they are within their best-before date, both the compressed blocks of fresh yeast and the various dried yeasts will generally work. Tim Hayward is used to the huge bricks of yeast utilised in the bakery he runs in Cambridge. He says it is one area where it pays to check the date on the packs. The fresh blocks need to be kept in the fridge, but they dry out quickly.

Even with dried yeast, though, it's worth putting a bit into tepid water with a pinch of sugar to check it bubbles if you've had it for more than a month.

Both Tim and Sue Lawrence prefer using fresh yeast. Sue's lived in Scandinavia and Germany, where fresh yeast is sold in every supermarket. For her, there's an emotional fix in handling it. It is deeply tactile, crumbling in your fingers, with a distinctive smell that she describes simply as 'wonderful.'

Meanwhile, Zoe Laughlin offers a cautionary tale. There are yeasts, and there are yeasts. Peckish at a boozy gallery opening, she once approached a table full of plates of handily sliced pieces of bread. There were people all around it talking, so she snuck her arm through and managed to grab a piece of bread. As she chewed, the entire congregation turned to her and someone piped up with 'Oh, can you eat it?' The artist happily informed everyone that yes, technically it was edible, but the yeasts were from her feet and her armpits.

That's Easter sorted, time to hastily move on. There are quite a lot of other days in the month and the lamb leftovers won't feed us forever. We all love a good crowd-pleaser, so here's to soup, a topic that regularly crops up in our inbox or is asked about by our audience.

Soup

Soup's a real mainstay of British cuisine. Emerging from the pottages and broths of the medieval era, it gained both its name and modern meaning in the sixteenth century. The word relates to 'sop' – as in 'soak' – and 'supper' and similar words exist in many other languages. The Italians have *zuppa*, the Germans and Danish have *suppe* and the French *soupe* (and *souper*). It's a huge category of foodstuffs, encompassing everything from stand-your-spoon-up-in-them winter warmers to the clearest of consommés. Well into the twentieth century soups were obligatory for the upper-class table, but also a mainstay of the poor. They can be made with store-cupboard ingredients or herbs plucked that instant from a dewy field. Truly, like *Kitchen Cabinet* episodes, there's is a soup for all seasons.

Is there a better chilled soup than gazpacho?

April isn't really the month for a hefty lentil rib sticker, so let's look forward to the summer when the grass is brown and the tomatoes are red. Gazpacho is the classic chilled soup, originating in Spain, but popular much more widely. Rachel McCormack says the secret to a good gazpacho is really, really good ingredients. Don't rush out now and buy supermarket tomatoes, restrain yourself until June when you can get hold of the kind of tomato that scents not just the room it's in, but also the one next door.

True gazpachos use Spanish varieties of cucumber as well, less watery and more flavoursome than the average British ones, so if you are using a British cucumber, peel it and remove the seeds. You also need a red pepper, garlic, bread and a little bit of water as well as – obviously – very good tomatoes. Mix all of this together, purée it in a blender and then add in good extra-virgin olive oil and some white wine vinegar. Season with salt and pepper and chill well. Rachel does admit that most of the Spanish people she knows simply buy a good quality ready-made one, though.

Sophie Wright recommends nipping north from Spain and up into France to sample a vichyssoise. Another classic chilled soup, it's made with leeks, potato, chicken stock and cream, all stewed down in oodles of butter and garnished with chopped chives. She describes it as 'Very refreshing, very velvety, smooth, silky … and even better hot.' She first encountered it in Anthony Bourdain's *Kitchen Confidential* when she was just about to start catering college and says even the idea of it made her excited for her new career. Her mother, on the other hand, read the book and was horrified at her chosen path – as well as her liking for serving her vichyssoise hot.

If, like Sophie, you fancy a hot summer soup, Annie Gray suggests another French soup, a jardinière. In classical cuisine, jardinière is a specific set of vegetables used for a garnish – carrots, turnips, French beans, flageolet beans, green peas and cauliflower – but it was also used as a name for a light soup based on the same elements. It's just a very clear consommé with lightly blanched vegetables added to it. The originals use chicken or veal stock, but a clear vegetable broth works just as well.

Annie says it is particularly useful for the opposite of vegetable gluts, as it is perfect for when the vegetable patch yields only a handful of peas, some slightly bird-pecked beans and a few roots you rescued from the slugs.

I batch-make soups for the week for lunch, but I'm invariably bored of them by the end of the week. Is there anything I can do to jazz up my soups?

Andi Oliver says yes, lots, and it's worth keeping a soup-pimping arsenal in your fridge. Try things like chimichurri, a blend of herbs and spices popular in Uruguay and Argentina. A bit like souped-up pesto, it's based on finely chopped garlic and deseeded red chillies mixed with minced parsley and oregano, all blended with olive oil and vinegar.

Then there's the Middle Eastern schug (or zhug). Andi uses coriander leaf, parsley, a bit of jalapeño or other chilli, along with cumin, garlic, spring onion, chives and oil. She just blends it up and keeps it in a jar.

Ramen offers a lot of inspiration for souping up soups, says Tim Anderson. His go-to is crispy fried shallots, made by slicing shallots very thinly and putting them into cold oil. Heat this gently and, as it starts to sizzle, keep the heat moderate so that they dry out without burning. Once they caramelise, drain on a paper towel and leave to dry. Fried onions are amazing not only for the bittersweet, savoury flavour they give, but also for the different textures: crispy, then chewy, then melty and soft.

Let's wade into the ring: ***How to make the best bacon sarnie***

Tim Hayward is very specific. Four rashers of thick-cut, dry-cured back bacon cooked in the oven at 180°C and packed into bread fried on one side only in bacon fat. The fried side faces in. He adds just a little brown sauce or ketchup.

And finally, we asked the audience about their most alarming restaurant experiences. Among many hair-raising tales, the standout was a small place in the 13th arrondissement in Paris. Our intrepid diner enjoyed a fine meal, and then nipped off for a wee. The loo was round the corner and not exactly near the restaurant. Not only was it a toilette turque (a squatty) but it was small on space. Having dexterously managed to do what she went for, she turned to flush and discovered a turd stuck mere inches from both the button and where her posterior had been but moments before.

Head buzzing? Here's a handy space to scribble down your ideas.

IPA
CUSTARD

May

This month's food fun includes:

Vesak Day (Buddha's birthday, time for vegetarian celebratory delights)

Artisan Cheese Fair, Melton Mowbray (300 cheeses, a true celebration)

Alresford Watercress Festival (featuring the Watercress King and Queen – a celebration of a bit of a forgotten leaf)

The World Pier Crabbing Championship (part of the Cromer and Sheringham Crab & Lobster Festival, what else?)

Eurovision Song Contest (love it or hate it, it's a brilliant excuse for a Europeanish-themed buffet)

Malton Food Lovers Festival (you have to admire a town that closes the whole of its centre in a good cause)

The moon this month is made of **Maroilles**

A washed-rind cow's cheese from northern France with its own AOP (appellation d'origine protégée), Maroilles is used in a lot of classic dishes from the Lille region, including tarte au Maroilles and endive gratin. It is usually described as having 'character', i.e. it is eye-wateringly stinky, especially the Vieux-Lille variety. It's in season from May to August and requires a five-week maturing period to reach peak pong.

This month *The Kitchen Cabinet* is in **Birmingham**, known for its cultural diversity, its industrial heritage and as the home of Bournville, Bird's and balti.

Key flavours in May are **unforced rhubarb**, **elderflower**, **peas** and **broad beans**.

And we are also thinking about:

- The best way to enjoy lardo
- What to drink with spicy food
- Music to cook to
- Kitchen superstitions
- And whether tablets or books are best in the kitchen

Welcome to Birmingham, known once as the City of a Thousand Trades. Its geographical location at the heart of the Midlands made it ideally placed to boom as the UK's Industrial Revolution gained pace. Modern Birmingham is the most multicultural city in the UK, a fact reflected in its thriving food scene.

If your only experience of Birmingham is Spaghetti Junction and being lost at New Street Station, you're missing out. While it might be known for more conventional retail therapy, our panel was more interested in shopping for pigs' ears at the Bullring covered market. The waterways and roads that converged on Birmingham have long made it a hub for business and opportunity, and it's hard not to love a city whose heritage includes both custard and curry. We loved it so much, we've been back twice.

Top tip: *What to drink with a warming curry*

Nisha Katona says just because IPA (India pale ale) has India in the name, it doesn't mean it's a good match with spicy food. Don't be swayed by the fact it's served chilled, or that it's a long drink. It'll just enhance the sting of curry – and the flavour doesn't usually work either. Stick to something cooling, such as the yoghurt-based drinks popular in India itself.

Panellist pick: ***Music to cook to***

For some of us (mainly Annie), the Eurovision Song Contest this month is the highlight of the year. But what do the TKC panel like to listen to while stirring their sauces?

Tim Hayward bakes to the soundtrack of a film called *Big Night*, good for singing along to. Special mention to Cab Calloway's 'Everybody Eats When They Come to My House'.

Dr Zoe Laughlin says her anthem is 'The Baked Potato Song' performed by George Dawes on *Shooting Stars*. It's only right for the inventor of the Zoe Laughlin's Almost-Patented Baked Potato Method (see page 144). But, more generally, Northern Soul.

Shelina Permaloo shakes her hips to Fela Kuti, one of the creators of Afrobeat, and says he's been in the background of all the best food she's ever had.

Sue Lawrence is exacting. For a cheese soufflé, she starts with Mendelssohn's *Rondo Capriccioso*, which starts gently and picks up when you are beating your egg whites. Then it's Tchaikovsky's Pas de Deux from *The Nutcracker* while it bakes, and you finish with Amy McDonald's 'Let's Start a Band' as you serve while dancing in glee.

Jeremy Pang admits that his choices are curtailed by children and it's mainly the soundtrack to *Cars 3*.

Jay Rayner is all about the food-theme show tunes. He's even got a live jazz show based on them. Top pick? 'It Must Be Jelly ('Cause Jam Don't Shake like That)'. Well, quite.

Curry

Birmingham is renowned as the home of balti. It's a tricky dish to describe, for there are as many baltis as there are restaurants in Birmingham, and then some. In the audience for one of our Birmingham shows we welcomed **Aktar Islam**, co-founder of Lasan, a multi-award-winning Indian restaurant in the city's Jewellery Quarter. He admitted to feeling ambiguous about balti. It was born out of the restaurant trade in the late 1970s, and is named for the karahi-like metal bowl it's cooked in. (The karahi is a Pakistani cooking vessel, similarly shaped but made from clay or cast iron.) Made in Birmingham from stainless steel, the balti enabled restaurateurs to produce a quickly made, easy dish, cooked and served in the same bowl. For Aktar, it's a huge boon to hard-pressed chefs trying to make a profit in a notoriously competitive trade, but it does a disservice to the richness of Indian cuisine, as it's become synonymous with Indian food in the UK.

It's time we recognise that what we call curry is essentially an Anglo-Indian invention.

Balti is a hybrid, but then so is curry itself, its development typical of the way the British cherry-picked the foods they liked, but adapted them for their own tastes, as they ran rampant across large parts of the globe in the eighteenth and nineteenth centuries.

The first curry recipe appeared in print in Hannah Glasse's *The Art of Cookery Made Plain and Simple* in 1747, which means curry was probably in fairly wide circulation at least 30 years before. The word dates to the late sixteenth century. It came from the Tamil 'kari', which meant spiced sauce, but the British adapted it as a blanket term for anything from the whole sub-continent, regardless of style, region, ingredients, technique or flavour. The earliest Indian restaurants appeared in the UK in the late eighteenth century, catering to soldiers and merchants returning from India, missing the foods they'd come to love while abroad. They did differentiate between dishes – pilau, chutney and kedgeree all became anglicised at this point – but for the majority, curry became a catch-all term.

While freely adapting Indian food to suit tastes and ingredients back home, the British also influenced dish development across the areas they colonised. Anglo-Indian food thus became a thing in both countries. Sumayya Usmani says it's not all bad. One of her favourite dishes, from neighbouring Pakistan, is called railway mutton curry. It evolved out of the spicy stews sold as street food at railway stations in the nineteenth century. The British loved the idea of it but couldn't cope with the spice. So local chefs kept the basic flavours of chilli, ginger, garlic, red onion, curry leaves and tamarind (which also helped to preserve it), but added coconut milk to dumb down the heat. It was ideal for travellers wishing to grab something interesting – but not too challenging – for a first-class carriage, for it could be cooked low and slow and served as required.

Many of the core ingredients of Indian curries were difficult to replicate in the UK, especially as the range of foods we ate dwindled. That's why you see apple or pineapple in place of mango or tamarind, beef for goat or mutton, and a range of pre-made curry powders, which were sold to those without an extensive spice cupboard from the eighteenth century onwards. But while some British curry recipes are undeniably a travesty (yes, the 1970s, we are looking at you), others can be great – as long as you recognise them for what they are.

Happily, in modern Britain we do now recognise that curry and Indian food are not one and the same. India is huge, with a rich and varied set of regional cuisines. Nisha Katona says the specificity of the spice mixtures used in each region is one of the things that really differentiates the food of India from generic British curry.

Different areas of India use different headnote spices. In Kashmir, for example, it's all about warming sweet spices. They're often used in a blend of sweet and savoury.

Asma Khan makes a walnut and apple chutney with cinnamon, cardamom, fennel and Kashmiri chilli, which is glorious with cheese. Or take Gujarati cuisine. Nisha brought along some asafoetida, a typical Gujarati spice, which is actually a resin. It's pretty pungent, known sometimes as the devil's dung. When cooked, it turns into a sort of butter, with all the creamy notes you'd expect, plus hints of onions and garlic. In some forms of Hinduism, onions and garlic are forbidden, especially for widows, because they are seen as heat-giving, passion-inducing foods. So, asafoetida is a really useful spice.

Gujarati food is very ingenious, says Nisha. It's primarily vegetarian, verging on the vegan, mainly due to the influence of Hinduism, as well as Jainism. In Jainism, no living thing may be killed – so even root vegetables are out as by taking them up by the root, you are killing the whole plant.

If you want to try something typically Gujarati, Nisha suggests seeking out dhokla, a Gujarati savoury cake, made just with gram (chickpea) flour, semolina and slightly fermented yoghurt. Once cooked, it's simply dressed with tempered mustard seeds, cumin seeds and curry leaves. She brought some to the show. Andi Oliver described it as 'gorgeous': light and incredibly fluffy and balanced beautifully with the sour note from the yoghurt.

Can the panel advise me on a really good fish curry? Mine always come out like a sludgy mess and I'm a bit scared to keep trying them.

Nisha Katona says for more complex flavours, cross the continent from Gujarat in the west to Bengal in the east, bordering Bangladesh. It's on the coast, so both freshwater and sea fish are widely eaten. She recommends a fried yoghurt curry sauce.

Fish in curried yoghurt sauce

Prepare yourself: you're going to deliberately curdle some yoghurt. It's a really liberating thing, and you should embrace it. Fry some nigella seeds and a green chilli in a little bit of oil. Add in some yoghurt, loosen with a little bit of water. Then just add your fish fillets, plus turmeric, a little chilli powder and some English mustard paste. Sounds crazy, right? Add something sweet to temper it – a good pinch of sugar is easiest –

and serve garnished with lots of fresh coriander leaf. Ignore what you read on the web, there should be absolutely no garlic, onion or ginger. Keep it simple, keep it authentic.

Andi Oliver relies on a curry paste she makes up and uses whenever she needs a quick meal. It's just ground cumin and coriander, turmeric, ginger, garlic and onions. She says it works really well with a firm white fish – just rub the paste all over and roast the fish to part-cook. Warm up some coconut milk, tamarind paste and some lime leaves – fresh or dried. Once the fish is almost cooked, pour over the sauce and let it sit in that in the oven for a further 10 minutes. The fish will crisp up, the coconut milk infuse – fragrant, subtle and lovely.

Time waits for no hungry panellist, however, so time to move on. Let's look at another Birmingham invention, and another British food favourite.

Top tip: *Eating lardo*

We spent a memorable evening in the basement of a beer hall in Leeds eating cold meats and cheeses and shouting about food. Tim Hayward taught us to put slices of lardo on our hands for a few minutes to warm them slightly. Lardo is very thinly sliced cured pig fat. It'll melt just slightly on your hand so when you then eat it, it instantly starts to melt onto your tongue, filling your mouth with flavour and glorious piggy goodness.

Custard

In 1837 Alfred Bird, an 'experimental chemist', opened a shop on Birmingham's Bell Street. His inventions included baking powder (sponge cake fans, feel free to shout hoorah), and an eggless custard powder, initially intended to help out Alfred's wife, Elizabeth, who couldn't eat eggs. He quickly commercialised his new product, opening a factory to produce a powder that remains one of the most well-known brands in the UK.

Custard powder is essentially just cornflour, colouring – originally turmeric, later annatto – and vanilla flavouring. All the canny cook needs to do is add milk to the desired consistency, and sugar to their personal taste. Unlike an egg custard, it's pretty foolproof, although when we asked our audience in Birmingham 82% of them told us stirring constantly was vital to avoid lumps.

But is it cheating? And if it is, do we care? It's not giving away any trade secrets to suggest that more than one member of the panel admits to adding a couple of spoons of custard powder to their egg custards, which stabilises and thickens them without the risk of curdling (plain cornflour will work just as well).

I grew up with my gran's egg custard, the most sublime pudding I've ever had, and I've travelled the world, but have never worked out how to replicate it. Please help.

Custard goes with tarts the way bacon goes with, well, the TKC panel's most intimate dreams. Dr Annie Gray says the name itself comes from medieval French: *crustarde* meant 'pastry', which was used, among other things, as an excellent way to consume custard, and gave its name to the filling after its older use was long forgotten. Everything set with eggs – flans, quiches, tarts, blancmange, set creams and, of course, custards – comes from that root. Consequently, Annie's made a lot of custard in her life, including a Tudoresque replica parterre garden, where the geometric shapes were made of enriched shortcrust pastry. Each was filled with a differently coloured custard.

Absolutely beautiful.

Tim Anderson says that for any custard you should get yourself a probe thermometer. Egg yolks coagulate at 70°C (the whites go at 60°C), but this temperature is raised when they are added to other things (like milk and sugar). The key is to keep your egg mix under 85°C, at which point it will scramble. Really, try not to let it get above 80°C. He also advises adding cornflour – but says be careful how much.

Mind you, if you do end up with a custard you can cut up and use as a doorstop, all is not lost. Just slice it and deep-fry it. The Spanish call it leche frita and Rachel McCormack says it is divine.

Custard comes up a lot. On our Stockwell show we spoke to **Antonio Luis** from Madeira London Patisserie, a purveyor of Portuguese custard tarts, or pastéis de nata. He uses puff pastry, and a custard based on flour, milk,

eggs and sugar, plus flavourings. Antonio wouldn't reveal exactly what he used – but we'd suggest vanilla and a touch of cinnamon. The secret, sadly, is a commercial baking oven, which reaches over 300°C, boiling the custard in its shell, baking the pastry almost instantly, and giving the tarts their customary blackened top.

Lizzie Mabbott points out that one of the side-effects of western European colonisation in the eighteenth and nineteenth centuries was to spread custard-eating to countries without strong dairy cultures. Macau, a former Portuguese colony, is famous for its egg tarts, which are similar to pastéis de nata, whereas Hong Kong, a mere 45-minutes drive away, has a more British-feeling egg tart. However, both are firmly rooted in Chinese culture, too. Lizzie brought with her some Hong Kong egg tarts (dan tat), which are made with a lard-based pastry, making it shorter and crumblier than butter-based forms. They are cooked lower than pastéis de nata, with a smooth, slightly alarmingly yellow filling. Apparently, it is totally natural, and useful for spotting them in a bakery window.

Custard: cold or hot?

All of these tarts and puddings revolve around baked custards, served well chilled. But hot custard is great too. Sophie Wright loves an old-fashioned custard-based pudding. Cabinet pudding, bread-and-butter pudding: bring it on. Rachel McCormack agrees. She puts whisky in her custard and spreads her bread with marmalade to take her bread-and-butter pudding firmly away from school dinners and stodge.

'Spotted dick and custard is delicious, or a roly-poly pudding. I think traditional puddings are having a bit of a revival.' – Sophie Wright

Andi Oliver makes savoury custards, great hot or cold. Just make a standard custard base – eggs, milk, boosted with cream – and then add loads of cheese. Her top tip is to cook it low and slow. A bain-marie in the oven is ideal. Just half-fill a deep roasting tin with hot water, and stand your ramekins filled with custard in that. It's a really gentle way to cook them and you'll get a wonderful wobble. Crème brûlées can be done the same way.

While we're on the subject, Tim Anderson has a custard niggle. He'd like to know the point of thin custard sauce. Thick or bust, quite frankly. Tim Hayward points out that thin custard sauces are often associated with the English abroad – zuppa inglese or crème anglaise – and he feels it's a bitter cross to bear. In fact, the panel are pretty united on this front. A custard sauce might have its place, but no one is quite sure where. True custard is thick. Jeremy Pang says the biggest mistake people make with custard is thinking of it as an accompaniment to other things. Custard is custard and the only thing it needs is a spoon.

Respectfully, not everyone agrees. Custard is indeed a fine thing, but there's one thing it seems made for above all else. Pink, sticky, versatile and brilliant right now, it is, of course, rhubarb.

Rhubarb

By now, the rhubarb fans among us will have been enjoying it for a couple of months. It's most often associated with the Rhubarb Triangle, an area between Rothwell, Morley and Wakefield, which was once so important in rhubarb circles that it had its own train – the Rhubarb Express, which took freshly picked stems down to London in time for the opening of the early morning markets. We spoke to **Janet Oldroyd-Hume** of E. Oldroyd and Sons, who've been growing rhubarb near Rothwell for five generations. She's known as the High Priestess of Rhubarb, an epithet we can all admire.

Rhubarb is a Chinese native, grown originally for medicinal purposes. Its thick, black stems were used as a laxative, usually dried and made into a powder. It wasn't until the eighteenth century that sweeter varieties were developed, which could be used as a vegetable or fruit. In the early nineteenth century, gardeners at Chelsea Physic Garden discovered the plant could be blanched or forced by being covered with soil and kept in total darkness. The resulting stems were sweeter, paler pink and more delicate – as well as much earlier – than those left to their own devices.

Annie Gray says **stories that the discovery was accidental are highly dubious.** The process was well known, and it's more likely the (highly skilled) gardeners were experimenting with a plant still seen as relatively exotic and interesting.

Janet explained the modern process for forcing rhubarb. It's grown in warm forcing sheds, in pitch black, well-fed and watered. They are fed with manure and shoddy, waste from the local cloth industry. The plants think it's spring and grow strong and fast. You can hear them grow (we listened to a recording). What little light there is comes from candles. Tim Hayward said he visited a forcing shed once and, between the low choral music, the candles, and the sound of quiet popping as the buds burst open, he wasn't sure whether he was part of an age-old food tradition or a remake of the *Invasion of the Bodysnatchers*.

'You can actually hear these things popping and, frankly, it was terrifying.' – Tim Hayward

By May, though you can still get forced rhubarb, the thicker, sharper stuff is bountiful too. When asked, 32% of our audience said it was best served under an avalanche of sugar and another 38% opted for honey and a bit of orange peel. When we think about rhubarb, most people's minds turn to sweet things. In fact, most people's minds turn to crumbles, and a crumble is, indeed, a fine and lovely thing.

But while *The Kitchen Cabinet* is always happy to help you to fine-tune a terrific recipe, we are also keen to encourage you to move beyond the obvious. Every year desperate gardeners, and friends of gardeners, and people who happened to pass by a gardener at the wrong moment, beg us for help with their rhubarb gluts. It's one of the things we thrive on.

I've only just learnt that rhubarb is a vegetable. What savoury things can I do with it to surprise my friends?

Sumayya Usmani recommends using it in place of tamarind. It's great in curries and with lentils and, while it doesn't have quite the same sourness, it does a pretty good job. Just soften it down with a little bit of sugar first. Annie Gray says she's not surprised it works as a tamarind substitute. She says you can also use it where you might use lemon. But what about a rhubarb soup? Very Victorian.

Rhubarb soup

Start with about a litre of really good beef stock, full of flavour, and throw in 6–8 stalks of rhubarb. Peel them if they are too old and hoary. Bring it all to a simmer and cook until soft. Add a couple of decent tomatoes or tablespoons of tomato purée, maybe a tiny smidge of shallot if you like it, and season. Stick it in a blender and serve with fried bread croutons. It is improved with fried bacon bits as well – either blended into the soup or served with the croutons.

Back to Janet, who supplies a lot of restaurants. She says it's often used with fatty meats like pork or lamb, or oily fish such as mackerel or salmon. Rob Owen-Brown loves using it like this. He suggests a jelly, made as you would redcurrant, to serve with roast game. Rachel McCormack puts it under roast chicken, but also makes a relish with chopped rhubarb, sugar, orange zest and juice and a couple of chillies. It goes with everything.

Tim Anderson goes a step further. He's a fan of home fermenting. Try peeling off the tough outer skin of your rhubarb stalks, chopping them up and salting them well. Rub them with cayenne pepper and layer into a bowl. Just weigh them down and leave them at room temperature for 4 or 5 days, pouring off the liquid as you go. Store in the fridge. It's good as an accompaniment, but just as good poured over rice. As ever with home fermenting, do be careful, and follow food safety guidelines.

The other advantage of rhubarb, not exactly a savoury dish but certainly not sweet, is as a pan-scourer. Zoe Laughlin points out that the same molecules that lend rhubarb its astringency in the mouth also make it an acid great for cleaning. Got burnt-on bits on your pan? Just boil rhubarb in it for 10 minutes and hey presto! Your stainless will be sparkling.

Don't rush straight to boil your pans though; stay with us for another of those thorny themes that just keep on causing you anguish. We touched on it when we talked about soup, but it's a stock question … no, really.

Panellist pick: *Superstitions in the kitchen*

Paula McIntyre admits to being superstitious about the number 13. An example? Oven timers. She can't set them for anything with a 13 in. Has to be 12 or 14.

Rob Owen-Brown has a thing about whistling in the kitchen, but he says it's older than him – talk to retired chefs and they'll agree: a misplaced whistle gets a crack across the knuckles with a ladle. Clearly, we don't endorse this kind of kitchen violence.

Do tablets have a place in the kitchen?

Annie Gray says no. How do you write on them? Make a recipe book a repository of your own memories? She writes in all of her books: what she did, who ate it and gets her dinner guests to write what they thought too. Books!

Tim Anderson says she needs to get a grip (or an app). He admits you have to turn off the screen timeout and keep your hands clean, but they're great. And if they get grubby, so what? Saves space, time and the world is there at the click of a keyboard.

Stock

Let's get one thing out of the way before we start. On behalf of all of us, Tim Hayward would like to rage for a few moments on the topic of definition. Stock is stock. If meat stock, it's made from meat with all its attendant collagen, gelatine and muscle, sometimes the bones, and usually a few additional flavours. They are cooked quickly to extract the flavour. Then the liquid is reduced to concentrate the flavour. So (here comes the rage), stock is not bone broth. You can't get any flavour from mere bones. So if you call your stock bone broth, stop it, and if you are genuinely boiling bones, stop that too. Celebrate the flavour and depth of proper stock. Broth might sound better on a menu, and that's fine, but if it's beef broth just call it that – nobody seriously wants to drink bone-flavoured water and, to be honest, nobody is actually serving that. Stock!

I'm confused by stock. Brown, white, raw bones or cooked? And how do I get that gloopy consistency chefs always seem to manage?

There's stock, and stock. It's had a lot of different names – broth, gravy, pot liquor – and there are lots of different grades. The modern definition of brown and white stock is very simple though. For a brown stock, whether it is veal, beef, lamb or chicken, roast your bones off first; for a white one, leave them raw.

Do you need a specific stock, or will a chuck-it-all-in and add some peelings approach do fine? Sophie Wright goes for a circular approach, beloved in restaurants.

Thus, if you are making a lamb dish, use the trimmings for the stock. The flavours will complement each other and you reduce waste. Jeremy Pang disagrees. His go-to is chicken stock, and he warns that rich game stocks pared with rich game can just be too much. Sometimes contrast is key.

Rachel McCormack says you need to think hard about what your stock is doing in your recipe. A lot of soups and stews don't really need a flavoursome stock because they have so much else to add flavour. She points out that the stocks you see on TV and encounter in restaurants are the result of prep chefs spending hours over a pot, cooking, straining and then reducing stocks for 18 hours.

There are cheats though – she advises sticking some Spanish cured ham bones into your pan, which will add instant flavour and save you some reducing time.

If you really crave a gelatinous texture and don't have a pan big enough to make a few gallons of stock and reduce it down to a mere litre, Tim Hayward is your man. He says it's all in the choice of meat. Modern stocks almost always include bones, so opt for the ones with lots of gelatine in them. If it's a chicken stock, go for wings, legs and feet, anything flexible with cartilage and collagen. For an instant fix, he buys a load of pigs' trotters, boils them up to release the gelatine, strains the liquid and then reduces it to a thickish jelly. Frozen in ice cube trays, you've got a load of little squares of instant jellifier – just pop a couple out and add them to any stock to get that silky smooth feeling you associate with great stock.

All of this is great, says Jocky Petrie, but you can't really beat spending time on a stock. He recommends a pressure cooker. It gets to a higher temperature, cooks for less time, and gives much more flavour than boiling in a standard pan. You don't lose any of the aromas of the stock, and the result is thicker and more glutinous straight away.

I've recently started eating a more plant-based diet, but I'm really struggling with stock. Ready-made stuff is too salty, but when I boil vegetables everything just seems to taste like cabbage.

Tim Anderson says it is all about the umami. A well-reduced meat stock has it in spades. But it's hard to get the right flavour into vegetable stock. Try cheese rinds – Parmesan and other mature cheeses have enzymes in that break down proteins into amino acids, one of which is called glutamic acid. Combined with the salt in the cheese, it makes monosodium glutamate, MSG, which is one of the most naturally umami-rich things around. Just boil the rinds down, and then remove them (you can try using a blender to purée them, but he says it's pretty dreadful).

Lots of foods are high in the all-important umami so crucial for stock. Tim uses dried mushrooms a lot, but also kombu (Japanese seaweed). Jordan Bourke suggests adding some miso for a bit of texture – you won't get the gelatinous feel of a meaty stock, but it will help. Xanthan gum is a more cheffy trick to achieve a similar result.

Jordan also has advice on the thorny topic of clarification. The problem is the way the process removes so much flavour, which you then have to add back in. If you do fancy having a go, it's best done while your stock is still very liquid and cold. All you do is mix egg whites (and sometimes the shells) with minced vegetables and meat (if a meat stock), pour them into the pan, and very, very slowly bring it to an almost-simmer. If you're making stock for an Asian-style soup, Jordan says use lemongrass, ginger and garlic. Count on another couple of hours. The egg will coagulate and bind to the impurities in the stock, forming a gritty, eggy raft on top of the pan, which can be carefully removed before yet more straining. Tired yet? You still need to reduce it.

Andi Oliver says she loves the look and feel of a beautiful, clear consommé, and that part of the joy is knowing how long it took to get there, but also admits she's not sure it's worth the faff. It's one to admire in restaurants, but probably not a thing to regularly try at home.

And finally, we asked our audience in Hull about their most hallowed kitchen rules. Apparently, spoon segregation is a thing. Respect to the audience member who refuses to let his porridge spoons be used for savoury dishes and finds himself locked in an ongoing battle with his daughter, who claims blithe ignorance. Rob Owen-Brown suggests he should invest in a spurtle.

Here's a handy space to doodle, draw or design a menu.

MUSTARD

June

It's officially summer! Other things to get us glowing:

Late May Bank Holiday, plus an extra holiday for the Platinum Jubilee (cheese-rolling happens in Gloucestershire for the particularly cheese-crazy)

National Fish and Chip Day (deep-fried and proud)

Chinese Dragon Boat Festival (standing eggs on boats and eating zongzi glutinous rice balls)

Shavout (Jewish Festival of Weeks – dairy foods are key, including cheese blintz)

Wybunbury Fig Pie Wakes (pie rolling. It goes back 200 years – and 20, which was when it was brought back after being cancelled for unruliness)

BBC Good Food Show (some of us may be there – we can't promise, but it's always good fun)

Start of Wimbledon (until July 10th) (strawberries! Cream! Champagne! Also, some tennis)

The moon this month is made of **Cheddar**

One of the most globally famous cheeses, the name is generic, and the cheese can be too. But seek out a real Cheddar, ripened, scalded and cheddared (a stacking and draining process that takes its name from the cheese) and you'll never look back. Seek out Cheddars with a PDO (Designated Origin – UK protected) such as Keen's, Westcombe's, Montgomery's and Quicke's. As a hard cheese, it keeps and travels well, and is particularly good for slicing or grating for summer sandwiches.

This month *The Kitchen Cabinet* is in **Cromer**, on the North Norfolk coast. It's best known for its Victorian pier, where you can catch a show – but better still, catch Cromer crabs.

Key flavours this month are **mustard** and **mint**, the first of the **new season's potatoes**, plus **broad beans**, **radishes** and **raspberries**.

And we are also thinking about:

- Sitting on our sandwiches
- What goes well with strawberries

- What we'd put in a TKC time capsule
- The best way to eat noodles
- And the perfect baked potato

Welcome to Cromer, once a tiny fishing village but expanded to a bustling seaside resort by the late Victorians. We recorded in the theatre on the end of Cromer pier, home to the last surviving end-of-the-pier variety show of the great British summer, having fished (unsuccessfully) for crabs off the side first. The sound van has proudly displayed its stuffed soft-toy crab as a memento ever since.

But there's much more to Cromer and the surrounding coast than just its shellfish. The salt marshes are stuffed with samphire, and the fields inland are a multicoloured joy – purple lavender, yellow mustard and green and white mint. So, as we sweep into summer, let's heave a collective sigh of relief at the end of the hunger gap. Bid goodbye to brassicas and start your summertime feast.

Panellist pick: *What would best represent you in a TKC time capsule?*

Sophie Wright opts for Auguste Escoffier's *Le Guide Culinaire* (*A Guide to Modern Cookery*). First published in 1903, it remains the bible for classical cuisine. Sophie says it contains everything a classical chef needs to know, from mother sauces to meat and vegetable preparation. It's already stood the test of time for over a century.

Dr Annie Gray admits it's probably the candle salad she made for our Pangbourne show and which went down in infamy (a web search for 'Annie Gray candle salad' will reveal all). It was intended to showcase winter salads and was a 1920s American recipe – a bed of lettuce, on which was a slice of tinned pineapple with a banana perkily poked into it, a handle made from red bell pepper, and then a liberal squirting of runny mayonnaise, to look like, um, wax. The tip was topped with a cherry, of course. (Nobody ate it: we just stared in awe.)

Quick-fire question: ***Things that pair well with strawberries***

Prof. Barry Smith: Well, champagne is classic, and as an umami-rich wine it goes really well with food and is a good match with strawberries. But that's an easy win, so I'm going for grass. Seriously, we did some lab research thinking the most common association with strawberries would be cream, but no, it's freshly cut grass. In culinary terms, try making a strawberry shortcake with a white chocolate ganache made with a really grassy olive oil.

Anna Jones: I use up all the squishy strawberries from the end of the punnet by just roasting them for 10 minutes with lemon and black pepper. They make a sort of mush, which is great on yoghurt for a quick breakfast.

Top tip: ***The best way to eat noodles***

Tim Anderson is our Japanese food specialist. He even runs a ramen joint. He says slurp! Slurp with vigour and a great deal of noise.

'When I hear people slurping at my restaurant, it's like music to my ears because I'm thinking, oh yes, somebody knows what to do. Somebody gets it.'
– Tim Anderson

There's a reason beyond the sheer satisfaction as well: it's the best way to get broth and noodles in your mouth at once. So, if your shirt isn't splattered at the end of your meal, you're doing it wrong.

Crab

British crab is at its best from April to November, and it's fished in a number of places. But crab from Cromer has had a particular reputation for being sweet and plump since at least the nineteenth century. We welcomed **Julie Davies** from Cromer's Davies Fish Shop to the show. Although she denied it, she has a reputation as one of the fastest crab pickers in the East, so, obviously, we asked for a demonstration. It was fast, loud and left us open-mouthed in awe.

To pick (deshell) your crab like a pro, start by removing the claws. Crack them open and pick out the meat, setting aside to add to your white meat later on. The legs aren't worth picking – use them and the shell for stock. Now take the crab in your hand, grip and lift the main body shell off to reveal the meat inside. Take out the lungs (also known as dead man's fingers) and discard. **They aren't poisonous, just unpleasant.** Inside you'll find two types of meat: the brown and the white. Most of the latter is within the main body, which in Cromer is called the shickle. This is where the real skill lies. Julie describes it as a bit like a grapefruit, with lots of segments, from which the meat needs to be coaxed. It takes time (unless you are Julie), but it's worth it.

I love a crab sandwich, but can the panel convince me that brown crab meat has a role to play in it? I'm not even convinced it counts as meat.

Chef and restaurateur **Mitch Tonks** was on another of our seaside shows, this time in Dartmouth, and the idea that brown meat was inferior made him decidedly crabby. He reckons the brown meat has more flavour, describing it as tasting like the sea. His ideal crab sandwich is brown meat spread on one slice of bread, with mayonnaise on the other. Sandwich the white meat in between the two and take a big bite. It's even better done in brioche and seasoned with loads of freshly ground white pepper.

Andi Oliver doesn't like her crab sandwich to be too bready. She suggests using a slice of toast, spread with brown and white meat, and topping that with sticky boiled eggs (halfway between boiled and runny). She adds wild garlic mayonnaise, a little bit of pickle and tops it with a few sprigs of samphire. It's a sort of Scandi-inspired deconstructed crab sandwich.

If you want a truly showstopping crab sandwich, what about trying Paula McIntyre's version? She's based it on simple crab, butter and bread, but then elevated it.

Crab sandwich, and then some

Start with a basic soda bread with some spring onion run through it. Then make a beurre noisette by gently browning some butter with a little minced shallot. Chill it, and then bring it back to room temperature before whipping it hard. Add some fresh fennel fronds and a bit of lovage and tarragon. You can also add parsley. Then just layer this with your crab – brown for sweetness and white for texture. Serve on the bread like a bruschetta.

Rachel McCormack is unconvinced by any of this. She wonders why anyone would bother with a sandwich when crab is so sublime by itself. Her perfect seaside lunch? Forget the bread, just squeeze a bit of lemon into the dressed crab – and grab a fork.

'Crab, wine, lemon, that's it.' – Rachel McCormack

If, like Rachel, you're not crazy about crab sandwiches, what else might float your boat? Sophie Wright says there are so many delicious ways to cook crab that there really is something for everyone. Crab cakes, obviously, and crab with mayonnaise – like Rachel, she advocates doing less to it rather than more and eating it as fresh as you can get it. But you could also try a crab quiche. Just mix the brown and white meat and spread it in the bottom of a blind-baked pastry case, then top with a savoury custard mix. Serve it with chargrilled asparagus spears. Or make a saffron crab mayonnaise, roll it up in really thin crêpes and eat it chilled.

Andi Oliver prefers to riff around the crab-cake theme but suggests putting them into gyoza skins to make dumplings. You can buy the skins or use wonton pastry. Just mince up crab with spring onions, garlic, a touch of chilli, coriander and some lime zest. Put a spoonful of the mix into each skin, dampen the edges and crimp. The secret to a good gyoza is to fry and steam them through, so get the pan really hot with a bit of oil, crisp up your gyozas and then add a splash of vodka or sake and get a lid on, quick. Leave them for about 45 seconds and you should end up with a silky top, crisp bottom and a lovely vodka sauce.

If the sauce on that has you salivating, Tim Anderson says you can't beat a good bisque.

Normally a bisque requires an intense, much-reduced shellfish stock, but with crab you can cheat by using the brown meat. Just add it to a base soup, made of tomatoes and white wine added to whatever stock you have to hand. Blitz it up and you should have a fine-flavoured soup stock with a good texture. Then you just add your flaked white meat on top, plus some tarragon or dill. Easy and delicious.

We mentioned mayonnaise, and for over 150 years Norfolk has been associated with one of the staple ingredients of this crabtastic condiment. Colman's Mustard is no longer made in Norwich, but much of the mustard seed used to make it is still sourced from the East of England. So, from salty to spicy, what's the thing with this divisive yellow paste?

Mustard

Mustard heat, says Prof. Peter Barham, is not the same as chilli heat. It's perfectly possible to enjoy a bit of chilli heat but actively loathe the nose burn that comes from mustard. It's comes from a molecule called allyl isothiocyanate, which isn't in straight mustard seeds, but develops when enzymes in the seed get wet and start to act on other molecules. Once the allyl isothiocyanate appears, it acts as a defence mechanism, attaching itself to and triggering the pain receptors in our nerves. If you eat lots of chilli, you can desensitise yourself. You cannot do this with mustard though – it just keeps on burning.

There's a further twist as well. Dr Zoe Laughlin has a good experiment for you to do at home. Take some plain English mustard powder and mix a little up with hot water, and the same amount with cold. Try them both – the one made with hot water will be substantially less pungent than the one with cold.

So, if you are using mustard in a dish, she says always add it at the end to get the full benefit.

I grew up on English mustard, but I notice it's getting harder to find – it's all Dijon and American and Swedish these days. What's the difference? Do I need more than one?

Annie Gray says mustard is one of the oldest spices we still use. You'll find recipes for it in Roman cookery, and it's been used both as a flavour and a medicine. It was cheap, it was easy to grow and it seemed to be effective for all sorts of things. It went into footbaths for chilblains, was mixed with honey for coughs and, since it was hot, was rather inevitably seen as an aphrodisiac. In Britain for a long time the centre of the mustard industry was Tewkesbury, and then Durham, where a Mrs Clements perfected the idea of what she called mustard flour – which we now think of as English powdered mustard. You could also get 'made mustard', which is basically what we buy in jars.

'Mustard … doth mightily stir up bodily lust and helps the spleen and pains in the sides, and gnawing in the bowels.' – Nicholas Culpeper, seventeenth-century herbalist and physician

The mustards we now buy as Dijon are in many ways much more akin to the stuff we would have been making in the medieval era. Mustard then was made up with verjuice or fermented grape juice, and those from Dijon still tend to be made with white wine. In the UK we use vinegar, which is sharper and less forgiving. English mustard is less likely to be flavoured as well, while Dijon mustards can have all sorts of funkiness added in. They are softer and more useful for cooking, says Rob Owen-Brown.

English mustard powder definitely has its uses. Rob likes it sprinkled over scallops, which are then fried. It works with beef too, either sprinkled on a steak or over a roast joint before it goes in the oven. You can also add it to batter. Made up, it's a classic table condiment, and a teaspoon on the side of your plate or spread in a sandwich is an amazing thing. But it isn't as good to start off a mayonnaise or to thicken a sauce.

Tim Anderson is a fan of Japanese mustard, which is very hot, like English mustard. It's also got a bitter note to it. He mixes it with miso and stuffs it into lotus root to demonstrate to people that Japanese cookery really isn't all delicate flavours and gentleness. But he also likes Dijon mustard for a less intense and more balanced experience. He recommends trying the full range, not just English, Japanese and Dijon, but also Polish, German, Swedish and even American (though he does admit that the latter is essentially yellow ketchup).

Can I make my own mustard? Where do I start?

Zoe Laughlin advises you to start with the seed type. Black are a devil to grow and process, and not much used any more for making mustard, though they remain popular as a spice, especially in Indian cuisine. Brown mustard seeds are native to Europe and are the major seeds used in European mustards. Then there are white mustard seeds, which are much milder, and used for American-style mustards, usually with some turmeric to give them the bright yellow colour we associate with it.

Rob Owen-Brown makes his own mustard. He says it is definitely worth the mild faff, for you can get exactly the flavour you want. He uses a blend of brown and white seeds, soaked overnight in cold water so that when ground they will make a paste. His personal poison is pink peppercorns, which he simply adds to the mix, grinding it all down with a little honey, some salt and a bit of standard pepper. The colours look gorgeous, and if you don't grind it too much, you'll be left with a lovely coarse texture.

Of course, if you really want a spice challenge, you could try blending chilli and mustard. Andi Oliver brought us a hot sauce to try that reduced the panel to fiery tears and much blowing of streaming noses. Use English wet mustard, Scotch bonnet chillies roasted from fresh, turmeric, spirit vinegar – and some coconut sugar, which she gaily and rightly pointed out we wouldn't notice. According to Rachel McCormack, once her eyes had stopped watering, it was more complex than most hot sauces and 'It does have a really nice aftertaste ... eventually.'

If your tastebuds are tingling, you'll need something to go with your sauce. Something you can cook in as many ways as you can imagine, and then some more. Something that's a guaranteed crowd-pleaser and perfect right now. It's a British staple, it's a potato.

Potatoes

Old ones, new ones, blue ones, purple ones, big ones and little ones, there really is a potato for everyone. Peter Barham explains that there's quite a spectrum, but they are usually divided into floury and waxy. Essentially, it comes down to the amount of starch and protein. The more starch, the easier it is to make them fluffy, which is the key to roasting, chipping and baking. Waxy potatoes hold their shape better, making them superior for salads and dishes such as pommes dauphinoises, which rely on potato slices that won't fall apart. There are also all-rounders, including the Maris Piper, which was bred in Ireland in the 1960s and is the UK's most popular potato. Tim's family owned a chippy in Bristol (he still feels slightly peeved that it was his great-grandfather's name that went up over the door, and not that of his great-grandmother, who inherited the place). His grandmother later ran it, and family lore has it that she tasted some early Pipers, then stalked Bristol's greengrocers throughout the late 1960s to track down the elusive tubers wherever they were stocked.

Did the introduction of the potato revolutionise European diets?

Yes, but not immediately, says Annie Gray. The potato is a South American native, domesticated around 8000 years ago. It was quickly picked up and brought back to Europe by the early explorers, who noted its value as a food crop, especially given its keeping qualities.

Although its early spread is hard to follow, it first took root in Spain, spreading outwards only gradually (**and with little to do with either Sir Francis Drake or Sir Walter Raleigh**).

It was widely regarded as a curiosity by most people. Prevailing medical theory, the Doctrine of Signatures, held that nature provided clues as to medical properties in the look of things – and potato tubers looked suspiciously like the symptoms of leprosy. Cultivation was also challenging in the very different climate of Europe.

However, in the eighteenth century, a combination of scientific and botanic study, population growth, famine and, as ever, war, meant that the potato started to be taken more seriously. The Prussians promoted it heavily, a wonder food for the poor and for feeding prisoners of war. One such prisoner, Antoine-Augustin Parmentier, took the appreciation of spuds back to his native France, giving his name later to a number of potato dishes. And in the UK it was enthusiastically seized upon as a way to feed the burgeoning population. By the turn of the nineteenth century, its popularity was assured, on the tables of both the rich and the poor. In many ways it was the real fuel of the Industrial Revolution, at least until the 1840s. Then blight struck.

The Irish Potato Famine shone a stark light on the dangers of monocultures, especially when combined with the systematic exploitation of rural workers by rapacious absentee landlords. Around a million Irish people died, and a further million emigrated in desperation. Blight became a global problem, still driving potato development today.

What is the most mind-blowing thing I can do to a new potato, gastronomically speaking?

New potatoes are perfect right now. Many of them are the waxy salad type – Anya, Charlotte, Jersey Royal to name but a few – but 'new' really refers to any potato harvested when small and somewhat immature.

For the ultimate potato salad, says Sue Lawrence, add truffle. Make your own mayonnaise, but instead of using all neutral oil, make a third of it with truffle oil. Use that to coat chilled boiled new potatoes, and then shave over some extra truffle – white or black. It'll look, smell and taste fabulous. Less salad than showstopper.

If your tastes are for more simple flavours, Sue also suggests going Italian with trenette al pesto. Trenette is a type of pasta, and it's just a question of mixing it with whole baby new potatoes simply boiled, plus green beans and pesto.

Nisha Katona reckons you could blow a few minds with new potatoes done in an Indian way. Just boil the potatoes and then toss them in fried nigella and white poppy seeds with green chilli and coriander leaf and a pinch of salt.

Or try this easy side dish, which is one of the best ways to showcase a really freshly dug potato.

An excellent potato salad

Take fresh new potatoes and boil until just cooked through. Then you need some really good olive oil, lemon juice, chopped spring onions, coriander, salt and then acidity brought in with some pickles – Nisha favours capers. Unlike many potato salads, there's no butter, no mayonnaise, just carefully chosen and very potent ingredients. And you can serve it hot, cold or somewhere in between.

Some of you may be reeling at the thought of no mayonnaise, so let's turn to Tim Anderson. His Japanese potato salad involves half mashing, half whipping cold cooked potatoes until they are creamy. Add into that cucumber and carrot, both salted and then rinsed (this makes them tender, but still satisfyingly crunchy), and then add bits of ham or bacon. The final touch is Japanese mayonnaise, which is umami-rich due to additional MSG, and creamier due to using only egg yolks (and more of them) than western commercial mayonnaises. You can serve it as is – or in a roll as a sort of Japanese potato salad carb-on-carb butty.

It has to be said that the simplest way to serve your new potatoes remains one of the best: just boiled with mint and dripping with butter. It's a neat way to segue into our final theme this month, for mint is another thing you'll see in the fields of Norfolk, grown mainly for making into mint sauce. But herbs more generally are making their presence felt right now. Gardeners will be eyeing up the sage triffid and ruing their placement of the rosemary. Worry not, we're here to help.

Top tip: ***The perfect baked potato***

We might have mentioned it a few times, but we're pretty certain that Zoe Laughlin's Almost-Patented Baked Potato Method (names may vary, the results stay happily the same) cannot be beaten. Wash your spud. Put a knife in about 5mm and score it all the way around the circumference at the widest part. Bake it at 150°C for about 2 hours (you can go higher and faster or lower and slower) and turn the potato over halfway through cooking. You should be able to see sugars just dribbling out. Turn down to 120°C and give it another hour (so 3 hours in total). The skin should be crispy, the insides buttery soft and – this is the best bit – because of your cut round, you can just twist gently and pull them open.

Panellist pick: ***A sandwich to raise the spirit (and fit easily in a bag)***

Sue Lawrence quotes the American food writer M.F.K. Fisher on a thing called a railroad sandwich. It's a long baguette cut end to end, with both sides slathered in butter, plus a smear of mustard, then filled with loads and loads of ham. Clamp the sides back together, wrap well in foil and/or a tightly wrapped cloth and then sit on it. Firmly. The ideal is someone with, shall we say, a fair beam, who will sit quietly without squirming (or, presumably, farting) for at least 20 minutes. The warmth of their body melts the butter into the bread, and the novelty will keep a child quiet for quite some time. If the name seems a little 1950s American, the alternative name is a bit more pithy: bum sandwich.

Mint and other garden herbs

North Norfolk's good for mint growing because of its very sandy soils. But mint is a problematic herb to buy and store – the leaves go black very quickly and it needs to be eaten pretty soon. Most of us are familiar with peppermint and spearmint – hairy-leaved types we can buy in supermarkets or watch go rampant in our gardens. But there are loads of varieties, from bergamot mint (tastes of Earl Grey) to strawberry mint (cute, good for garnishing) and chocolate mint (like mint choc-chip ice cream, but better).

Help! My mint's taking over my garden. What can I do with it beyond mint sauce and mojitos?

Don't dismiss the mojito, says Jordan Bourke: build on it. He recommends a mojito sorbet, which is just stock syrup (equal weights of sugar and water, heated to dissolve the sugar and then left to cool), mint and as much rum as you like. Whack it in the freezer and give it a stir from time to time. Unlike a normal sorbet it won't freeze solid, because of the alcohol, so you're aiming more for granita than true sorbet. It's truly refreshing and dead easy to make.

Mint sauce can also be a solid base. Paula McIntyre makes a version that is not only good as an accompaniment but can also be used as a rub for roast mutton or lamb. It's just lots of mint, some chilli, white balsamic and medjool dates, all blitzed up with olive oil. You get the tongue-puckering punch of the mint in vinegar, toned down with the sweetness of the dates and a little kick in the background.

Tim Anderson, meanwhile, favours shiso, a Japanese herb that is part of the mint family, but less invasive in the garden, and more complex in the kitchen. It's ubiquitous as a garnish in Japanese cookery and makes an excellent palate cleanser due to its lemony, minty, pepper flavour. He also suggests trying Vietnamese coriander, which is sometimes known as Asian mint, though it isn't related to the mints we are more familiar with. It tastes, he says, like coriander dialled up to 11.

We spoke to edible plant specialist **Chris Smith** of Pennard Plants. He's also a fan of Vietnamese coriander, which he finds particularly good with eggs. His other go-to is green ginger rosemary, which can be used anywhere you'd normally use rosemary, but is also great infused into a sugar syrup and used diluted as a drink.

My partner uses way too many herbs when cooking. It's not just the quantity, it's the clashing tastes and more is more nature of it. Can the panel help me curb this insanity?

Andi Oliver says tasting is absolutely key when cooking with herbs (well, it's pretty key generally, but in the case of adding strong flavours, you really can't correct it after the fact). Start small, build up. And start with one herb and get used to the way it works before you throw in everything you've got. Take dill, for example, which has become very popular off the back of Scandinavian cuisine but can be very strong. Andi says going to

Sweden in her teens was the first time she'd really seen fresh herbs being used in quantity, and a lot of it was dill.

If you want to start gently, be inspired by Swedish crayfish cooking, where the crayfish are simply boiled in water with dill in – the dill flavours without overpowering. Or how about dillkött, which translates as 'dill meat' and is usually made with veal shoulder or lamb. The meat is simply poached with dill stalks, stock or water, potatoes, celeriac, onions and carrots until it is tender. Strain the boiling liquid, make a roux and then add enough of the liquid to create a thick, lovely sauce. Then you just add a little vinegar, a little sugar and loads and loads of chopped fresh dill, and pop the meat and vegetables back in to warm through.

Tim Anderson also likes using dill for pickling, making a pickling liquid of vinegar and a tiny bit of water, sugar, salt, garlic and whatever spices he fancies at the time. But he says that while generally he'd always favour fresh herbs, dill is one thing it's worth keeping in your larder in dried form. It means you can recreate one of his favourite American crisp flavours. Just take a large bag of salt and vinegar crisps. Add dried dill. Shake that bag … and you've got a crisp that tastes like pickles. They are fantastic.

Another herb that is useful as a dried store-cupboard staple is sage. Sophie Wright warns it can be quite intense and is best used sparingly. But it works really well sprinkled over chicken or root vegetables when roasting, and it works especially well with squash. Why not try a butternut squash and sage quiche?

Sage and butternut quiche

Roast some butternut squash with dried sage and a bit of garlic and sweat off some onion with a bit more sage. Cool slightly, then add them to a basic savoury custard mix of double cream and eggs. Season, and put that into your prepared pastry base. It's even better with a pastry made with dried sage in it as well. Put some fresh sage leaves on top of the mix, and it'll not only taste lovely but look fabulous as well.

Generally, says Tim Hayward, the woody herbs lend themselves best to being dried – leafy herbs like parsley and tarragon are better fresh.

Rachel McCormack thinks rosemary is one of the most versatile herbs to have around. Fresh or dried, it works with any kind of meat, but it is also good with fish. And it works really well infused into milk, at which point you can use it not only in savoury dishes but also sweet. Think rosemary-tinted white sauce, cheese and rosemary tarts – or even rosemary ice cream.

And as the curtain closes, we asked our audience about their most memorable buffet experiences.

Unsurprisingly, the buffet horror stories beat the buffet highs. Our favourite was the Cromer resident who watched her partner reach for a handful of what they thought was peanuts only to discover they were, in fact, someone else's discarded olive stones.

And remember, we're always hungry to hear from you – so hit us with your comments, questions and your own culinary traumas via tkc@bbc.co.uk or #BBCTKC on social media.

If you want to be part of the show, simply head to the BBC Shows and Tours website and click on the link for tickets. You'll see TKC events pop up when we are about to start recording a new series. They're free, it's fun and we can't do it without you.

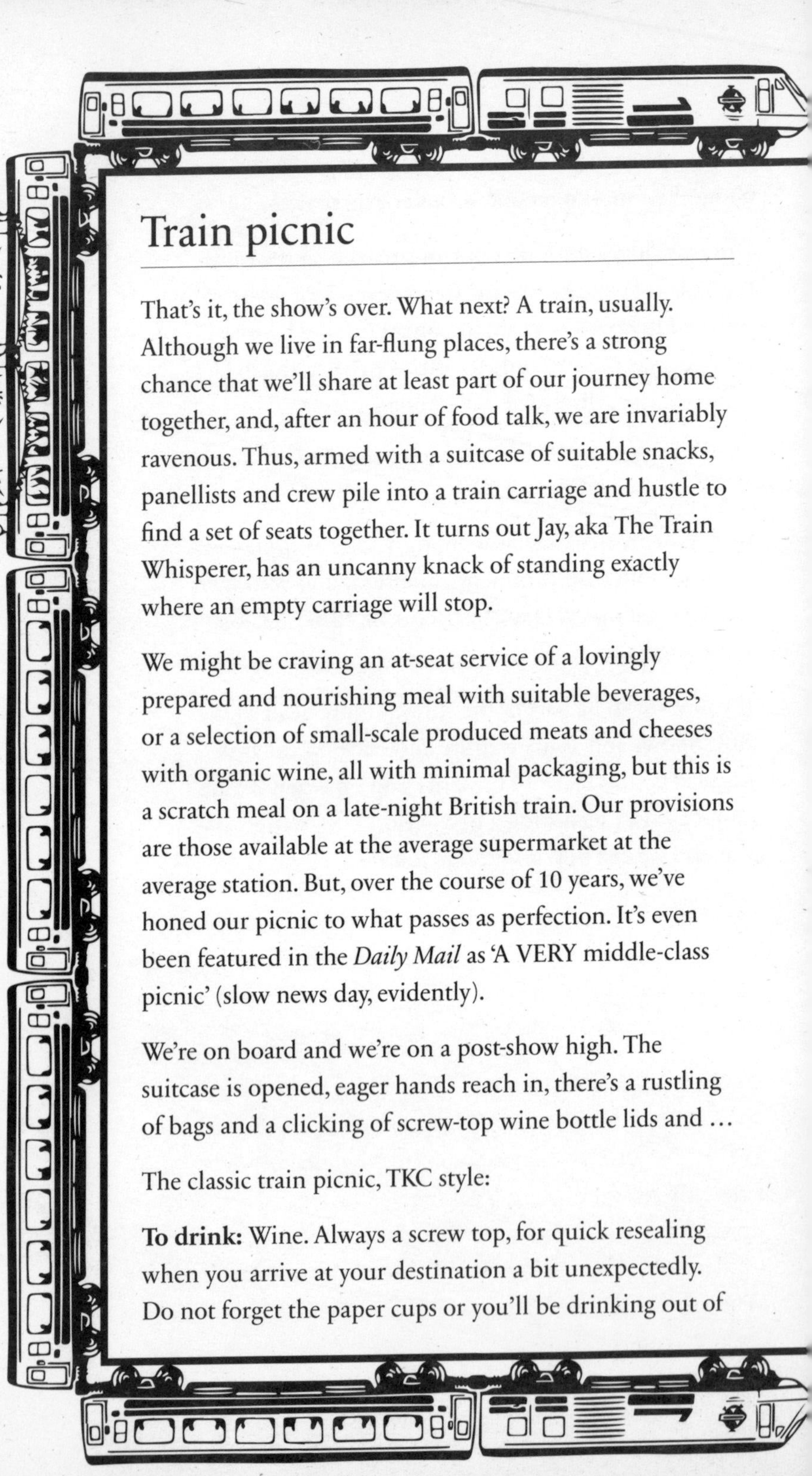

Train picnic

That's it, the show's over. What next? A train, usually. Although we live in far-flung places, there's a strong chance that we'll share at least part of our journey home together, and, after an hour of food talk, we are invariably ravenous. Thus, armed with a suitcase of suitable snacks, panellists and crew pile into a train carriage and hustle to find a set of seats together. It turns out Jay, aka The Train Whisperer, has an uncanny knack of standing exactly where an empty carriage will stop.

We might be craving an at-seat service of a lovingly prepared and nourishing meal with suitable beverages, or a selection of small-scale produced meats and cheeses with organic wine, all with minimal packaging, but this is a scratch meal on a late-night British train. Our provisions are those available at the average supermarket at the average station. But, over the course of 10 years, we've honed our picnic to what passes as perfection. It's even been featured in the *Daily Mail* as 'A VERY middle-class picnic' (slow news day, evidently).

We're on board and we're on a post-show high. The suitcase is opened, eager hands reach in, there's a rustling of bags and a clicking of screw-top wine bottle lids and …

The classic train picnic, TKC style:

To drink: Wine. Always a screw top, for quick resealing when you arrive at your destination a bit unexpectedly. Do not forget the paper cups or you'll be drinking out of your reusable coffee cups or, in extremis, an empty sandwich box. Turns out neither coffee dregs nor mayo work with wine.

To start: Crisps, many and varied, but really all anyone wants is salt and vinegar, and the weird roast beef and horseradish ones will always be left at the end.

Dips: Taramasalata and hummus are classics and not to be messed with. Provide breadsticks, along with a misleadingly labelled French baguette, which is strangely soggy but all they had.

Nibbles: The good old mixed meat platter where everything tastes broadly the same, plus Parma ham, because the thrill of peeling it off the backing strips never gets tired. Cheese is harder – blocks don't work because the knife is somewhere at the bottom of the suitcase under a load of question sheets and cheese squares are divisive. They will, however, get eaten.

Extras: Mini pork pies, stuffed vine leaves, those weird little crinkly cocktail sausages, which double as rubber balls, stuffed tomatoes and mozzarella balls and some olives. We are very fond of both vinegar and salt.

Sweet: Big tubs of chocolate cereal things, and a couple of packets of biscuits (also chocolate). If you plan carefully, there will be enough room in the tub for the bits left uneaten and someone can bear it away as a prize at the end.

The TKC twist: We may be lucky and have saved a few things back from the show to supplement these riches. We usually put the food we've prepared out for the audience, along with anything brought by our local food contributors. But sometimes things are just too good, and over the years we've picnicked on spider crab, alfajores, honey and cheesecake, to name but a few. Then there's the ultimate train picnic ... a really good fish and chip shop at the station.

BUTTER

July

Days to delight in this month include:

Foodies Festival (nationwide events throughout the summer)

Independence Day (USA, but still a good excuse for an election cake and a very serious BBQ)

World Chocolate Day (enough said)

Pontefract Liquorice Festival (who doesn't love a tongue stained black?)

National Ice Cream Day

Whitstable Oyster Festival (little salty morsels of joy)

The Yorkshire Dales Food & Drink Festival (big, hilly, delicious)

Welsh Wine Week

Caerphilly Big Cheese Festival (music, medievalism and a great cheese race)

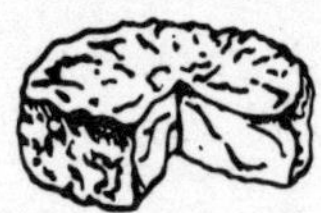   

The moon this month is made of **Tunworth**

A British Camembert, described by Raymond Blanc as 'The best Camembert in the world', and as far removed from the highly uniform produce of the industrial Camembert factories as can be. Available all year round, it nevertheless varies with the seasons. Summer cheeses come from cows fed on pasture, winter ones from cows fed on silage. Incredible baked.

This month *The Kitchen Cabinet* is in **Belfast**, known for all things *Titanic*. Not just the doomed liner, which was built here, but also the epic Ulster fry, bringing together a lot of Irish classics on one gloriously laden plate.

Key flavours this month include **butter**, **strawberries** and **samphire**, plus **cherries**, **runner beans** and **sea trout.**

And we are also thinking about:

- Feta on the barbecue
- How to shell quails' eggs
- Crisp sandwiches

- Places of personal culinary significance
- And how to make the perfect mash

Welcome to Belfast, where striking modern sculpture meets Victoriana, all overseen by some very big cranes. Once known as Linenopolis, it's been the capital of Northern Ireland since partition in 1922. We've been to Belfast twice, and the panel has eaten very well indeed. We won't name the panellist who stayed an extra few hours claiming it was for the *Titanic* exhibition, when really it was all about the potato farls.

Top tip: *Feta on the barbecue*

Anna Jones recommends feta as a barbecue showstopper. Just wrap the whole 200g block in foil along with some cherry tomatoes, oregano, sliced garlic and roasted peppers (from a jar is fine). Grill it or tuck the package into the dying embers for 10 minutes or so. A kind of magical alchemy occurs ... just taste and smile.

The Ulster fry

The UK is known for its breakfasts, but while we might all thrill to a plate of bacon and eggs, there are important regional differences. The Ulster fry is an icon, and certainly not to be confused with its cousins, the full English, full Welsh or full Scottish. There are shared components. Paula McIntyre says yes to bacon, butter and an egg, maybe to some mushrooms, tomato and black pudding, and a hard no to baked beans. The key Irish elements are soda farls, preferably fried, and potato bread.

Big cooked breakfasts can be divisive. Tim Anderson admits he's not keen on the traditional 'full' anything. There's just too much on the plate. But he has a fix: the breakfast burrito. Hash browns, sausage, bacon, scrambled egg, tomato, mushrooms and beans – they all work in a wrap. Plus, says Tim, you can really go all in with the sauces. Brown, red, hot chilli – do it all. You get the taste of a cooked breakfast, but in a convenient handheld format.

'Look, this is basically a public service, what I'm suggesting here.' – Tim Anderson

For a lot of people, breakfast cereal remains a quick fix for time-pressed mornings. But there's a dark side to the cereal story. The earliest breakfast cereals were developed in America, by figures such as Sylvester Graham and John Harvey Kellogg. They were Seventh Day Adventists, and believers in a very rigorous lifestyle, lots of cold baths and austere foods and stints in health sanatoriums. They promoted vegetarianism, abstinence, and the repression of natural urges, particularly sex. Cereals were part of a range of foods developed and marketed as healthy by the movement, but what they meant by healthy was bland and unstimulating. It gets much worse in the case of Kellogg, who was incredibly racist, a eugenicist, and performed some truly unpleasant experiments designed to stop any form of sexual pleasure.

When breakfast cereals were launched in the UK, most of this stuff was left behind, although the whiff of a moral agenda did worry people. They were also seen as eroding the sturdy British version of healthiness represented by the Great British breakfast (or at least by bacon and eggs, which was the most common iteration of it). But they were pushed as being glamorous and sexy and American. Still, one 1920s writer remarked, 'No-one who can get good porridge would ever want to eat those nauseating American proprietary breakfast cereals.'

I'm after a great breakfast-brunch in bed. Something with no crumbs, and that will say 'I love you,' and 'I'm really sorry about that thing.'

Whether it's to demonstrate love or ask for forgiveness, or simply for the sheer hell of doing it, a breakfast in bed can be a great thing. Sue Lawrence says if you just want something simple and crumb-free, porridge is it, obviously. But it isn't sexy, so what about a bagel? Crumb-free and it can be embellished to a level of greatncss. How about smoked salmon and cream cheese?

Sophie Wright is also keen on a low-crumb baked good. She opts for croissants, made into croque-monsieurs. It's easy to do – just slice the croissant across, fill it with a really cheesy béchamel sauce (Gruyère is best), add a slice of ham and top with more cheese and bake. It's even better if you make loads, pile them round a plate and crack some eggs on top. Just serve it as a big, creamy, cheesy sharing plate.

Even if your bread tends towards crumbly, you can fix it. Jordan Bourke likes a savoury French toast. Sourdough bread, dipped in eggs and cream, really well seasoned, fried and served with bacon, roast tomatoes, avocado and maybe some kimchi.

That's all rather knife and fork-led. If you prefer something more handsy, Tim Anderson would like you to think once more of the breakfast burrito. But if you aren't keen on the full-cooked breakfast idea, it's remarkably versatile. Try one with huevos rancheros, the classic Mexican dish. Normally it's fried eggs on corn tortillas with red salsa, pinto beans, avocado or guacamole. But if you scramble the eggs and add a lot of cheese … maybe a hash brown or two … it's not only a crumb-free breakfast, but pretty good for a hangover cure as well.

While we don't advocate drinking to the point of desperation the next day, we all admit accidents happen. If it's a hearty hangover cure you are after, Rob Owen-Brown goes with potato fritters. If you really are in a state, you could even do it with packet mash.

Potato mash brunch fritter

Mix up your mashed potato with some chopped black pudding, parsley, salt and pepper and mould it into a sort of hockey puck. Flour it, egg it and breadcrumb it and then deep-fry it. While it's getting brown, poach some eggs. Serve your potato cake with a poached egg on top, some hollandaise or Béarnaise sauce. If black pudding doesn't do it for you, it's also good with smoked salmon or finnan haddie. Beautiful.

Eggs are a winner, agrees Jeremy Pang. He opts for a Chinese dish called a jian bing, which is basically a Chinese crêpe, made with a mixture of mung bean and plain flours (you can use plain if you can't get mung bean flour). It's usually served just with sweet bean sauce and chilli sauce, but it's great with a couple of eggs cracked on top as well. And it's even better served with deep-fried wontons or (his personal predilection) a couple of frankfurters.

Nisha Katona advises adding something with a punch. Whether it's to wake you up as you perch on your pillows, or get you going when you're mildly regretting the night before, she suggests adding Indian pickles. You want pickles without onion or garlic, so you don't taint your mouth. But other than that, you can use pretty much any vegetable. She uses a spice blend of fried mustard seeds and fried fenugreek seeds added to untoasted mustard seeds, all ground, plus lemon juice and mustard, a pinch of sugar and salt and some rapeseed oil. Add in some green chillies for a bit of a bite.

Panellist pick: *Places of personal culinary significance*

Sue Lawrence: The kitchen in Provence where I was an au pair one summer when a student. I learnt to use aubergines and to make vinaigrette. It was a kitchen of true merit.

Jordan Bourke: My mother-in-law's kitchen and farm in South Korea. She makes her own gochujang, which takes months. Some of the best meals of my life have come from there.

Dr Zoe Laughlin: A windswept beach, which makes the fish and chips taste all the sweeter.

Rob Owen-Brown: A particular shellfish shack in a well-known Scottish port. Super-fresh fish, an ocean view, and the heavy diesel fumes of a big Scottish trawler. I've been known to drive 350 miles just to get my fix.

Top tip: *How to shell quails' eggs*

Andi Oliver admits she struggled for years, but then someone told her the vinegar trick. Just soak your boiled quails' eggs in vinegar – she uses white wine vinegar – for 8 to 10 minutes. The shells will slip off, and they won't taste of vinegar as it's purely on the shell, which you've removed. It's absolutely brilliant and utterly foolproof.

Butter, butter, buttermilk

We mentioned soda farls, one of the key tastes of an Ulster fry. But what are they? Paula McIntyre explains that they are a loose dough of buttermilk, bicarbonate of soda, bread flour and salt. It's divided into pieces, flattened and simply cooked on a griddle, having been scored through lightly so it's easy to tear into four triangular pieces. It's crucial that you keep the dough well-floured and don't handle it too much, for all the rising comes from the alkaline soda reacting with the acid buttermilk, and it's easy to accidentally knock the air out. Farl originally meant the fourth part of a thin cake made from oatmeal or flour. The best farls are flavoured with the nutty taste of slightly scorched flour from your griddle. Paula says that traditionally a goose feather was kept handy to brush off the surface between buns.

I buy buttermilk to make Scotch pancakes, but then I don't know what to do with what's left. Can the panel help please?

Tim Anderson points out that what we now buy as buttermilk is a cultured product made from milk. It's useful in baking, but nowhere near as versatile as the real thing. In fact, if you don't have buttermilk, you can fake it with two-thirds full-fat yoghurt to a third whole milk. Tim uses it in dressings to add acidity and says that the classic American ranch dressing is based on buttermilk.

Buttermilk is really useful for another American icon, says Sophie Wright, southern fried chicken. She soaks the chicken in buttermilk first to tenderise it. Rob Owen-Brown agrees but adds a Mancunian twist. He recommends using rabbit, jointed, soaked in buttermilk for 24 hours, patted dry, and then floured, egg-washed and covered in breadcrumbs laced with English mustard powder. Deep-fry that and you have crispy fried bunny.

You can use cultured buttermilk pretty much as you would yoghurt, says Andi Oliver. It's great in a marinade, such as tandoori. Just throw in some chilli or paprika, garlic, cumin, coriander – all lovely things – and marinade the meat in that. She recommends putting the spiced buttermilk in a bag or plastic box, chucking in some chops and leaving them overnight. When you grill or barbecue them the next day, they will be tender and the buttermilk will have created a lovely crispy coating.

It's slightly different if you can get proper buttermilk, i.e. the liquid that comes off when you churn cream to make butter. Dr Annie Gray says that for much of the past most country houses had their own dairies, and dairying was very much a quotidian activity. Buttermilk was used very widely, in scones, breads and baked goods, but also in rather more left-field ways. It was recommended for stain removal, specifically blue ink. Apparently, says Annie, it does work.

Back in the modern world, Sue Lawrence points out that the real thing makes a refreshing drink, still very popular in Scandinavia today. It is particularly good very chilled and served with hot cardamom buns.

I bought a small butter churn recently and it's fun, but I'm not sure my butter really tastes any better than the ludicrously expensive but amazing butter I buy from my local deli. What can I do to boost my butter, and stop my family telling me to chuck my churn?

Butter is both satisfying and easy to make at home. But it takes time, and it is very hard to get all of the buttermilk out, so it does go rancid rather fast. Prof. Barry Smith says this is why most butter in the past was salted, often quite strongly. Salt is an antimicrobial and stops the bacteria growing by depriving them of the liquid in which they can multiply. When it comes to cooking, most historic recipes assume you are using salted butter – unless they call specifically for sweet (unsalted). Our panel is more divided. Jordan Bourke says he likes to control the salt levels, so uses unsalted and then adds salt; Paula McIntyre uses salted for savoury and unsalted plus salt in cakes, and Rachel McCormack speaks for most of us and just uses salted for everything.

If you want to do something different with your butter though, there are definitely options. You could smoke it. Fifteen miles south of Belfast, **Allison and Will Abernethy** hand churn Abernethy butter. Along with salted and unsalted, they also make a smoked butter. They wouldn't tell us exactly what woods they use to cold smoke it, but if you have a cold smoker, it's something you could try. Rachel McCormack says that yes, you could then cook with it, but frankly you could also just eat it in slices. Paula McIntyre agrees that you don't need to do much with it. It gives a smoky flavour

to whatever you add it to – so is perfect poured over steak while it rests or stirred through vegetables. But she also browns it, adds some whisky, and folds it through a custard base before making it into ice cream (on the show at this point we had a small pause while the panel stopped drooling on the microphones).

The Abernethys also make flavoured butters, using local ingredients such as dulse (seaweed). Tim Anderson is a big fan of a flavoured butter. Surprisingly, the Japanese have quite a strong butter tradition, which came out of nineteenth-century government-led attempts to modernise and quite deliberately westernise.

Tim suggests making ponzu butter, made with lime and soy sauce, or spicy miso with miso and chilli. Andi Oliver, meanwhile, opts for a more traditional herb butter – wild garlic and spring onion. Her top tip is to add a bit of olive oil when you blitz it all together in a blender, as it helps to keep it together.

You can make sweet butters, too. Annie Gray went foraging in the history books and introduced us all to fairy butter.

Fairy butter

All you need is about 200g butter, a hard-boiled egg yolk, a dash of orange flower water and a heaped tablespoon of caster sugar. Beat it all in a mortar, and then comes the cool bit. You want to put your mixture in a dishcloth – the old-fashioned knitted kind – and squeeze it so it comes out of the holes like little yellow curly worms.

What it has to do with fairies is anyone's guess, but it's nice on a bit of brioche or a pancake.

Top tip: ***The perfect crisp sandwich***

Andi Oliver: The right crisp is crucial. Use a Hula Hoop or other ring-shaped potato snack. Plain. Then you need a decent amount of butter and a sort of gentle compression. Not too much or the crisp will poke through the bread, but not too little or it's impossible to eat.

Paula McIntyre: Taytos are an iconic Irish crisp. When they've been airmailed to you abroad and consequently turned to dust, and are then sprinkled into a sandwich with cheap sliced white and butter, they are a proper taste of home.

Tim Hayward: 'You are all barbarians; what is wrong with you? Chase me with pitchforks if you will, but the whole idea is utterly appalling.'

Annie Gray: The addition of a crisp to a sandwich is her go-to hack for terrible shop-bought sandwiches. Crisps add flavour, texture and about the right amount of seasonings, which such sandwiches always lack. She opts for a crinkle-cut salt and vinegar if she can. Crushed hard.

Picnics

We're in July, a month of wall-to-wall sunshine, long evenings and the start of the summer holidays. All right, we admit that the sunshine is frequently lacking, that the evenings tend to get buggy and the school holidays wear thin quite rapidly, but still, even in the UK it's time to break out the baskets and roll out the rugs. Love them or hate them, picnics are part of summertime living.

The modern picnic emerged at the end of the eighteenth century, says Annie Gray. It was the coming together of two strands: the basic worker's meal and the medieval and Tudor idea of aristocratic hunting feasts. On the one hand, bread and cheese by a haystack, and on the other, tables, cloths and some very fancy food. The word picnic appears in the UK in the Georgian era, along with a certain romantic notion, all Byronic posturing on craggy hillsides and exploring ruined abbeys, pie in hand. But the word is French and started off meaning a sort of pot-luck, a highly Rousseau-esque egalitarian feast where everyone brought a dish.

Inevitably, the Victorians codified it, always up for a bit of class-defining etiquette, and it mooched on as something that could be plain or fancy until we hit the 1970s and caravanning took off. That's when picnics really became what a lot of people think of them as – gingham cloths, things in plastic boxes, sand, ants and reliance on convenience food. Books of the time extol the virtues of things in tins – one of Annie's favourite horrors is chocolate Swiss-roll slices topped with tinned pineapple, squirty cream and grated chocolate. But that was probably the nadir, and we've come a certain way since then.

Love picnics, hate soggy sandwiches. What are the panel's showstopping dishes for al fresco dining?

Rob Owen-Brown says forget picnicking without a pork pie (see December). Dead easy to make, and the only thing he'd consider carrying miles into the countryside. Make it a gala pie, and it's even better. The hot water crust is basically indestructible, and if you make your own you can bask in the glory that pie always brings.

Sue Lawrence suggests a stuffed sourdough loaf.

Picnic loaf

Just cut the top off a loaf, scoop out the middle, and smear the inside with pesto or tapenade. Then layer up your fillings. Start with vegetables: marinated peppers, tomatoes, artichokes and rocket all work. Add a layer of cold meats, such as Parma ham or mortadella, and then some cheese – feta, mozzarella, maybe sharp Cheddar. Keep going, end with a drizzle of olive oil, put the lid on, wrap it very tightly in clingfilm and weight it down in the fridge overnight. It'll be solid enough to travel and cut into colourful, showstopping wedges.

Annie Gray goes with very Victorian cold roast meats. But how about a 1970s twist – a chicken crapaudine, which is spatchcocked by cutting under the breast but over the legs, and then flipped out? Your chicken will have a kind of waist, with the wings pointing forward and the legs backwards, like a small creature. Grill it – you can add a rub for extra pzazz – and when you serve it, garnish it with a couple of slices of hard-boiled eggs and black olives for eyes on the front. No one will forget you in a hurry.

If all of that is just too, well, large, Tim Anderson suggests onigiri, which are basically rice balls, a lot like Italian arancini. Onigiri means 'to squeeze or clutch', so it's really just rice squeezed into a pyramid shape. They're usually filled with pickles or meat or, in Hawaii, Spam, where they are known as musubi. Tim made some for us, delicately wrapped in nori (seaweed), which has the added benefit of keeping your hands from getting sticky.

Picnics are about more than just the food though. There are rituals to be observed. Every family has their own: groundsheet or rug, wicker or plastic, cutlery or fingers: it's a minefield. Tim Hayward has Opinions. He vividly recalls childhood picnics trekking over sand dunes following his laden-down dad while the family sang the theme tune to *Lawrence of Arabia* behind him. Then the arrival on the beach, the squeezing into a space between a hundred other sweating fathers, dog poo pushed to one side. And the sandwiches, wrapped in plastic wrap for just long enough to really get soggy, and for the inevitable slice of tomato to force its way through the marge into the bread.

'It was the most profoundly dispiriting eating experience of my life. I do not do picnics and I never will.' – Tim Hayward

Prof. Peter Barham says there are certain tips that will help. A portable fridge, for example, made simply from a terracotta flowerpot. Soak it really well and turn it upside down. As the water evaporates, it'll suck heat from inside the flowerpot, taking the temperature down by several degrees. If, on the other hand, you want something to stay hot (I mean, it is British summertime), pop a handwarmer inside and the trapped air will get surprisingly hot – certainly up to 40–50°C.

The last word on picnics might have to go not to one of our panellists, but to the anonymous editors of the 1880s edition of *Beeton's Book of Household Management*. They give a long list of things that can go wrong, from badly arranged transport to people who don't get on, forgetting the salt, the bread or simply providing little choice of victuals. The phrase to strike terror into any good Victorian's heart though? 'An abundance of wine and no corkscrew.' Just watch the panel shudder.

Ice cream

It's hot (maybe), it's sunny (possibly) and the tinkling of the ice-cream van haunts our every waking moment. It's a topic we cover regularly on *The Kitchen Cabinet*, our panel nobly sacrificing themselves to scoff sorbet and cram themselves with cream ice in the name of advising the nation.

The history of ice cream is much longer (and cooler) than you might imagine. Peter Barham explains that it all hinges on the discovery that by adding impurities to ice, you can get its temperature below freezing. You can use anything, but key to the development and success of ice cream was the addition of salt. Ice was being harvested and stored in ice houses around 6000 years ago, and the use of ice mixed with salt to freeze liquids seems to have been established at least 2000 years ago. However, modern ice creams emerge from Italy during the sixteenth century. By 1619, James I was keen enough to have an ice house built in the park at Greenwich. Inevitably, there are lots of myths flying about – but **ice cream has nothing to do with Marco Polo, Catherine de Medici or gunpowder manufacturing.**

I don't need any more kitchen gadgets. But how do I make ice cream without an ice-cream maker?

The use of just ice and salt to freeze ice cream remained the norm until the 1950s. Peter Barham carried out an experiment on our unsuspecting audience. He ladled some ice-cream mix – in this case a rather luscious Victorian cucumber ice – into a tough zip-lock bag, then put that bag into another, and then in another, and then put the double-bagged mix into a larger double bag filled with crushed ice and lots of salt. (He then put the whole lot into a laptop bag in case of accidents.) Our audience proceeded to throw this enthusiastically from person to person to churn it. It has to be admitted that they could have been more enthusiastic, as it wasn't quite as smooth as it could have been, but it did start to freeze. You can replicate it at home by burying a double-bagged ice mix in a bowl of ice and salt, removing it every 10 minutes or so and giving it a really good pummel. Or use a lidded metal container – a tea caddy is ideal – set in the ice, which you can twizzle and open to stir well.

Paula McIntyre suggests making a granita. You can do it with anything, but fruit purée is standard:

Basic granita

Start with a sugar syrup (100g sugar and 100ml water), add about 500g fruit, such as mango or strawberries, and purée it all in a blender. Stick this in the freezer and then just fluff it all up with a fork every hour or so while it is freezing.

Andi Oliver builds on this by using ready-frozen fruit, which you can just blitz up with a bit of sugar syrup and maybe a pinch of salt, some fresh herbs or, even better, a splash of vodka. It's pretty much an instant sorbet.

You can just use ice, adds Tim Anderson. If you've got a powerful enough blender, blitz plain ice and then pour cold coffee over it. Or use tomatoes and Worcestershire sauce, and a touch of hot chilli sauce – add that to your vodka and add the ice back in and it's a Bloody Mary granita. In Japan, the technique is used for kakigōri, literally 'shaved ice', which is mentioned in Japanese literature from the tenth century. For that, you use a special machine, which gives you a pile of ice like a snowdrift. Then you pour a sweet syrup over it – he likes to use yuzu-flavoured milk or matcha green tea syrup.

If all of that seems reassuringly simple, Jocky Petrie points out you can always use liquid nitrogen. He was part of the team at The Fat Duck when it became known for its nitro ice, but it was first suggested by Agnes Marshall, a late Victorian recipe writer and innovator who quite a few of the panel regard as a forgotten food hero. Peter Barham was part of the development team at The Fat Duck and says the mouthfeel is quite extraordinary. Liquid nitrogen is around -196°C and makes ice cream in about 10 seconds, meaning that the crystals that form are incredibly small and the resulting ice cream smoother than anything you can achieve by other means.

Can the panel convert me to savoury ice creams?

When ice creams were first introduced, they were served as part of the dessert course and intended as palate cleansers. Sweetness didn't necessarily follow – after all, this was a course that by the end of the Victorian era also included cheese savouries. Agnes Marshall published recipes for moulded ices made of curry, spinach and a very punchy devilled lobster iced soufflé.

Jocky Petrie says don't dismiss the idea. The team at The Fat Duck not only made sardines on toast into an ice cream, but also did a burger ice cream with tomato ketchup jelly. Although most of them didn't make the public menu, they did become well known for a mustard ice cream served with red cabbage gazpacho and a crab bisque ice. Jocky says a lot of the appeal lies in the mixture of textures and the contrast of hot/cold.

Peter Barham agrees. It's all about context. He says one of the best things he's ever eaten was Melba toast with a bit of anchovy on top, and a tiny scoop of smoked tomato ice cream – it had creaminess, smokiness, salt, sweet and crunch. Annie Gray – another fan of Agnes Marshall – suggests that if you can't get your head around savoury ices, try making them into a starter. She serves an eighteenth-century Parmesan ice cream with a slice of melon, some Parma ham, black pepper and a bit of basil oil.

There's really nothing you can't make into ice cream. In our Hay Festival show we met **Juliet Noble** of Shepherds Ice Cream, made, you've guessed it, with sheep's milk. It's very high in solids, meaning the milk can be used with no need to separate off the cream. It's therefore lower in fat while still being satisfyingly creamy – the same is true of goats' milk ice creams. Juliet likes to experiment with tea and coffee flavours, including a spiced chai and a cardamom. They'd be as at home at the start as at the end of a meal.

So, what are you waiting for? (A space in the freezer, possibly.)

How to make the best potato mash?

Jordan Bourke says get the right potato. Always floury: he favours Yukon Gold. Cut them into same-size pieces so they cook evenly and place them in cold salted water, which you then bring to the boil. Drain them properly and then put back into the hot pan to steam for 10 minutes to get rid of all the water. You only want to add butter, not water, to your mash.

Niki Segnit says you can bake them and scoop the mash from the skin. Then you add good-quality butter – like any simple dish, it is all about quality ingredients.

Jordan uses a normal potato masher for a slightly lumpy finish, but you could use a ricer for very smooth. Do not under any circumstances use a food processor unless you just want potato glue.

And finally, we asked our audience whether they lived to eat or ate to live.

In Pangbourne we met a couple who openly admitted she was obsessive while he was … less so. In our guise as couples' counsellors (it happens more often than you might imagine), we suggested embracing it. She gets to plan and cook and not suffer interference from a man who will eat pretty much anything; he gets to sit back and enjoy it. Count your blessings (even if a sneaky fish-finger sandwich means a subtle bit of subterfuge).

Busy looking up recipes on the web? Here's a handy space to write them all down.

August

What's hot in the calendar this month:

International Beer Day (followed by the Great British Beer Festival in London)

St Oswald's Feast Day (largely defunct, but worth reviving: in Grasmere it meant gingerbread and rush-strewing; in Lincolnshire it was rush-strewing and tosset cakes)

Afternoon Tea Week

Devon Street Food Festival

Late Summer Bank Holiday (barbecues at the ready

Newlyn Fish Festival (all the fun of the fin)

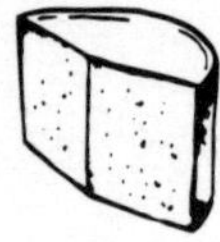

The moon this month is made of **Kirkham's Lancashire**

Lancashire is another classic British cheese bastardised by mass production into a form quite unlike that which it had for most of its life. For those familiar with the mass-market crumbly versions, as reliable as they can be, the older form is a bit of a (delightful) shock. It's made slowly, cutting and pressing the curds over a day, before mixing them with older curds and pressing them into a final form. Young Lancashires are mellow, older ones more punchy. Mrs Kirkham's is the only remaining producer of raw cow's milk Lancashire cheese.

This month *The Kitchen Cabinet* is in **Dartmouth**, known for seafarers, seafood and Devonshire cream teas, taken with expansive harbour view.

Key flavours this month include **tomatoes**, **French beans** and **basil**, **plums**, **sweetcorn** and, of course, **grouse** (the season opens on August 12th).

And we are also thinking about:

- Good reasons to have a microwave
- Our most aggravating food sounds
- Some school holiday science projects

- How to tenderise octopus
- And why you shouldn't keep your tomatoes in the fridge

Welcome to Dartmouth, a living postcard on the mouth of the River Dart. While most people head here to sun themselves on a beach, pick up a paddleboard or ramble in the Dartmoor National Park, our panel were keen to head to the harbour. Its medieval fortifications form a backdrop not only to manoeuvres from the Naval College, but also to the fishing fleet, bringing back crab and other such goodies for us all to feast on.

Top tip: *Tenderising octopus*

Tim Anderson likes to barbecue octopus for many, many hours, both to tenderise it and give it a smoky flavour. Leave it for long enough and you get octopus jerky. Rob Owen-Brown agrees with slow-cooking: 3 hours in a chorizo-tomato-winey sauce. Dr Annie Gray gives it 20 minutes in a pressure cooker. Sue Lawrence says she gives it to her Greek next-door neighbour, whose mother used to take it out to bash it against rocks to get it tender.

Afternoon tea and scones

We caught up on crab back in Cromer in June, and while we are always happy to revisit a firm favourite, Dartmouth – and Devon – have another claim to gastronomic fame. Nobody on the panel is exactly averse to a bit of butter and we're pretty keen on cream as well. We couldn't come to Dartmouth and not talk about tea. Afternoon tea or cream tea, cakes, scones and sandwiches, we'll eat it all. So, bring us a three-tiered cake stand, and let's get stuck in.

Annie Gray tends to pull faces whenever afternoon tea is mentioned. She says one of the most pervading myths in food history is that afternoon tea was 'invented' by Anna, Duchess of Bedfordshire, in 1842. **But think about it. A date that exact?** For a practice that was very clearly going on for at least 150 years before then? We've got so many pictures and texts that reveal that people were having a pick-me-up cup of tea with a light snack from the early seventeenth century onwards.

Even the term was recorded in the late eighteenth century, but it wasn't widespread until the last quarter of the nineteenth century, and therein lies the clue.

Giving a widespread practice a name and then bigging up a vaguely cool-sounding invention myth with aristocratic connections is classic Victorian. Add in some rules – milk first, cream first, where to put your spoon – and you've got a brilliant way to test people's social skills and then judge them for their behaviour.

Annie could (and has) gone on for hours on this topic. But in the spirit of the Victorians, she says tea titbits should be bland and tediously stereotypically feminine, as tea was heavily feminised. Light sponge cake, jam tarts and never a scone in sight.

Controversial, and naturally Tim Hayward disagrees. His go-to is all about the décor. Never mind the past, modern afternoon tea is about the rituals. The cake stand. The pot. The crockery. A sense of occasion. If you get that right, you can do whatever you want: macaroons, sandwiches, cakes and definitely a scone with jam and cream.

The scone-tastic Devonshire cream tea was popularised by the region's tourist boards, who saw an opportunity to take a thing with a whiff of the upper crust, reinvent it to highlight a truly regional product, and sell it to the newly motorised tourists of the twentieth century. Cream teas are a great thing, and clotted cream the defining product.

Prof. Peter Barham explains that despite the debates we are consciously avoiding, there really isn't (or shouldn't be) a difference between Devonshire, Cornish or Jersey clotted cream. Yes, the taste in dairy products changes with the diet of the cows, but with modern feeding techniques you're not going to suddenly get a cream that tastes of onions. He points out that the technique to make clotted cream was invented hundreds of years ago and was widespread across the globe.

In the audience we welcomed **Nicholas Rodda** of Rodda's clotted cream. He talked us through the process of making it. It's vital to have high-fat milks, which are

put in a centrifuge to separate out the cream. It's baked gently until the crust forms and then chilled. It means you have a pasteurised product, which is full of flavour from the cooking, and slightly concentrated to boot. Before pasteurisation was common for milk products, this gave it a real edge for selling, as it was safer than raw milk and kept for longer. His family started selling it in the 1920s, and never looked back. Nicholas says that for him, the key ingredient for an afternoon tea is friends or family. Scarfing a scone on your own just doesn't quite do it.

My scones fail. Every time. Please help.

We asked our audience in Dartmouth whether it should be jam or cream first and it was inconclusive (loudly so). Apparently, the Devonshire way is cream first, but mutterings from the panel and audience alike suggest this may just be made up in the name of regional rivalry. Successful regional rivalry to judge from the shouts from the floor. Andi Oliver solves it for us all by suggesting butter then jam then cream. Double dairy, and it stops the jam sliding about.

Anyway, what does the order matter if your scone isn't succulent? Sophie Wright says the most common issues are not enough baking powder and too much kneading. A scone dough isn't bread, so don't overwork it. And get it in a good, hot oven.

Jordan Bourke suggests using buttermilk, the Irish way, but with butter as well, to get a good texture. Andi Oliver agrees, adding that you can also use sour cream or yoghurt. She likes a savoury scone: a sharp Cheddar cheese, jalapeño chilli, walnuts.

Getting the cheese right in scones can be a challenge. Prof. Barry Smith advises against strong Cheddar and prefers Parmesan. For a successful cheese scone, you need to hit your eater with the smell first, and Parmesan is excellent for that.

Meanwhile, Itamar Srulovich flies in the face of the TKC's ongoing butter love-in and opts for margarine. He does a feta and Cheddar scone, where the margarine makes the scones short and less buttery, so that the cheese flavour really sings. Rob Owen-Brown challenged us even further, with his butter-free scone: 300g flour, 150g yoghurt, bicarb, salt and a pinch of sugar. We tried them. They were, it's fair to say, a brave effort.

Finally, a word of warning from Barry Smith. Snacking between meals is a slippery slope. Your glucose levels are dipping mid-afternoon, and you boost them with a bit of sugar. The insulin kicks in, your blood sugar levels then drop, and you head toward hypoglycaemia. So, you need a bit more of a hit and you get to the point where you either need to go for a run or just keep eating. And it's fair to say, it's pretty easy to do the latter. His advice? Remove temptation. If the biscuits are there, you'll reach for them – it's what psychologists call facilitation behaviour. You have been warned.

Top tip: ***Good reasons to have a microwave***

Tim Anderson: It's great for steaming vegetables, useful for checking the seasoning on stuffings and meatballs while the mix is still raw (quick blast in the microwave, no need to dirty a pan with frying bits) and it is the only good way to reheat lasagne and risotto.

Sue Lawrence: It stews fruit really well. With apples it's fast, and with rhubarb it helps retain the shape and colour. Reheating or melting chocolate too. Just not steaming puddings – they are lovely for about 5 seconds and then they just go hard and horrible.

Sophie Wright: I didn't have one until I had a baby and now I couldn't live without it. Plus, let's face it, if you've eaten in a pub or restaurant at all in the last 15 years, you've enjoyed a bit of what it's brought to food service.

Barry Smith: Just don't reheat your coffee in it, that's all. It can explode. Don't try it at home.

Sandwiches

Like it or not, the chances that you'll be scoffing sandwiches this month is high. A prime choice for picnics, travelling and simple lunches in the sunshine, they're a staple for the home cook and grab-and-go alike. The history is pretty clear: an obvious idea, eaten for aeons, given a spruce up and aristocratic name in the eighteenth century. The story goes that John Montagu, the 4th Earl of Sandwich, was at the gambling table one night, decided not to stop for supper, and ordered instead a bite of beef between two slices of bread. **The truth is murkier** – Montagu was perennially broke and a workaholic, not a big gambler, and his idea didn't come out of nowhere – he'd almost certainly seen pitta breads used with a filling on his travels in the eastern Mediterranean, and workers had been sticking stuff into hunks of bread for basically ever. However, the thing was certainly named after him, and the term spread like wildfire.

What sandwiches can I make to guarantee no complaints from my pernickety kids and their equally fussy friends?

Sandwiches are divisive. Angela Harnett says the key is contrast. She likes a meat filling with pickles, so sweet and soft, crunchy and acidic. Tim Anderson agrees, and suggests a classic Reuben: rye bread, sauerkraut, melted Swiss cheese, salt beef and a bit of Thousand Island dressing. It's crunchy, crispy, acidic, meaty, salty, cheesy – everything you want, in a handy bun.

Sophie Wright reminds us that the classics are classic for a reason. She's a fan of a crusty white bloomer filled with lots and lots of salted butter, crumbly Cheddar and what she terms a 'moist-maker': pickle, piccalilli, that kind of thing. But rarely salad.

Cheese is a definite crowd-pleaser. Another obvious one is ham. Jordan Bourke grew up on ham sandwiches and says it wasn't until he moved away from Ireland that he truly realised how exceptionally good they are. Their beauty lies in their simplicity, with a filling of nothing more than salted butter and freshly boiled ham, cut into slices. Slices with a heft, he points out – a centimetre thick is ideal. (He also recommended we look for Mícheál Ó Muircheartaigh making a ham sandwich online for a bit of understated excellence in the way of sandwich-specific content. It includes the classic line 'Bread was never meant to be triangular'. Enjoy.)

Andi Oliver is a bit scared of ham heft. She suggests a medium-sized cob loaf, properly crusty on the outside, with a lovely fluffy centre. Toast it just enough so that it can support the amount of salted butter you need to spread on it, i.e. a nice thick layer. Then she adds thinly sliced ham – not the slightly sweaty supermarket stuff, but just as thin as you can carve it at home. Electric carving knives might be weird but they are also pretty helpful here. Then it's just lots of strong English mustard, baby gem lettuce, job done.

If you can't decide between hefty ham and chiffon-like charcuterie, what about a good sausage? Tim Hayward recommends poaching the sausages in lots of oil at a very low temperature and sticking them in a flatbread with plenty of brown sauce. He says 45 minutes is about right for cooking the sausages (and claims it really helps a brutal hangover, although nobody was quite sure they'd cope with a 45-minute wait when they were feeling that bad).

Itamar Srulovich suggests slicing the sausages lengthways and then frying them, cutting down the time considerably. He also suggests soaking the bread in the frying medium. Rachel McCormack disregards all of that. She says you should just get a train to Glasgow, buy a Lorne sausage (a square patty made of sausagemeat), grill it, stick it in a Glasgow roll, which is a bit like a ciabatta with a crusty top, add plenty of brown sauce and thank her later.

Cheese, ham, sausage. It's fair to say that nostalgia plays a part in making the ideal sandwich. Sumayya Usmani's favourite is a sandwich her granny used to make. She'd use leftover beef keema – a spiced mince dish – plus red onion and chutney, all put between two slices of white bread and toasted in an old-fashioned stovetop sandwich maker. It would come out steaming hot but crunchy from being fried. To be eaten fast, before it went soggy.

How do I stop my sandwiches getting soggy?

It's all about the build, says Sophie Wright. Especially if you plan to take it with you, you need to consider the structure. Use a leaf – and a substantial one – to stop the filling from soaking into the bread. You cannot have a moist-maker touching the bread, so that barrier is key. Spinach, lettuce, endive all work – even the much-maligned iceberg lettuce comes into its own. But, whatever you do, never, ever use a sliced tomato.

Dr Zoe Laughlin takes a different approach. As a materials engineer, she's keen to promote the stuff of carrying as well as the stuff of stuffing. Plastic boxes are great for preserving a sandwich's integrity, but then you end up lumbered with an object that needs carting about and takes up loads of space. Clingfilm is more useful, but environmentally dubious. Foil is better, as it will mould around whatever you need it to, squish small for easy carrying afterwards, and can be recycled. Cloth impregnated with beeswax is also a popular option for those looking to reduce their use of plastics.

But there are other, newer technologies. Zoe showed us a 3-D printed fabric, inspired by the Japanese art of furoshiki, which is all about wrapping things (beautifully and properly) in cloths. In Japan, furoshiki cloths are used for clothing, bento boxes and presents. Cloth breathes and absorbs – but of course also leaks. Her cloth is a mixture of nylon and glue. It's still a work in progress, but she describes it as being a little like chain mail, with articulated links that can be designed to bend in certain ways. The eventual idea is to have a fabric that is fully flexible but then becomes a rigid box, so you can whip it out, fold it round a baguette and have a protective container for carrying it – which then folds into a tiny bit of cloth when you've finished.

Panellist pick: *Food science projects for the school holidays*

Zoe Laughlin opts for ice cream (see July). She suggests making it with yoghurt, banana and a bit of honey. Just nestle a metal container (or even a saucepan) in a bowl of ice and salt and have a go at it.

Tim Anderson goes for molecular gastronomy with a Hervé This recipe for chocolate Chantilly. If you melt chocolate into hot water in the correct ratios, it forms a similar kind of suspension in fat as whipping cream. You melt chocolate and water together in a saucepan, then you pour it into a bowl set over another bowl of ice water. And then, while it's still warm, you whip it. Stop at soft peaks: if you over-whip, it will split. As it aerates, it will chill and set. You end up with a delicious, really airy but also pure chocolate mousse. And it's fantastic.

Tim Hayward says just start a sourdough culture: delicious bread and a brand-new pet.

Aubergine

As we move into high summer, gardens and market stalls start groaning with seasonal fruit and vegetables. We are well-used to addressing your questions on gluts, and we are always here to help. This month's bounty includes aubergines, a vegetable (well, technically it's a fruit) that many of us love, but whose tendency toward sliminess can be off-putting.

Tim Anderson says it is one of his favourite ingredients, however, and one he'd happily write a recipe book on. From baba ghanoush to pepping up pizza, it turns out the whole panel is in favour of embracing the aubergine, but yes, there are certainly things to be aware of.

I've always salted my aubergine, but under the influence of *The Kitchen Cabinet* I'm starting to question everything I've ever been told about food. So, please, should I keep on salting?

Barry Smith says that historically aubergines were purely ornamental. The fruits were just so bitter that nobody would have considered eating them. They only became popular (ish) in the nineteenth century, and they were still pretty winceworthy. Salting them helped draw out the bitterness. But modern varieties aren't as bitter, so it doesn't really apply as a reason any more. However, you might still want to salt them if you object to the oiliness when cooked. Salting draws out the moisture and changes the cell structure, so they won't be as absorbent.

Sophie Wright agrees. Salting does firm them up. But in most cases, the point of aubergine is the melty, soft texture. Tim Anderson reckons it makes little real difference in most cases but does point out that some aubergines are still quite bitter. He uses little white aubergines, which look like eggs. In America, aubergines are still called eggplants after this type, which were probably the first to be used widely. But for the common UK purple beasts, he wouldn't bother.

Aubergine – why?

If you remain unconvinced about aubergine, let us convince you. Tim Hayward says the Sicilian caponata is absolutely gorgeous. It's made from cubed aubergine along with celery and onions, all fried in loads and loads of olive oil to really get a heavy, rich oiliness. Then you add capers and pine nuts, tomato sauce (or tomatoes), sugar and vinegar. Some versions use raisins as well. You end up with a kind of sweet and sour, cold pickle stuff, with crunchy nuts and soft aubergine. It's just as good cold as hot. And (though he hasn't tried) Tim reckons it would be great cut up into cubes, breadcrumbed and deep-fried.

Andi Oliver suggests halving them lengthways, seasoning with salt and pepper, and cooking them on a griddle brushed with oil until they start to collapse. Then get creative by smothering them with a sauce, which you can then bake. How about riffing on a satay – minced onions and coconut milk, thickened with ground peanuts and served with toasted peanuts on top? Or try mirin, chillies, shoyu (Japanese soy sauce), garlic, ginger, spring onion and toasted sesame seeds. Or head to the Med with smoked paprika, oregano, chilli, garlic and olive oil.

Jordan Bourke agrees that aubergine takes well to flavour. He opts for the Korean version, gaji namul. Just chop the aubergine into chunks, steam it, and then top it with a mixture of spring onions, sesame seeds, chilli powder and soy sauce and grill to caramelise. There's a Japanese take as well – nasu dengaku – done with miso.

Nasu dengaku

Slice your aubergines lengthways, score them and fry them on a medium heat for about 5 minutes on each side. Put a lid on them so they part-fry, part-steam and cook until they are squidgy and slumping. Put them on a baking sheet, fleshy-side up, and cover them liberally in a sauce made from about 100g miso mixed with a couple of tablespoons each of mirin and sugar and a teaspoon of sake (Tim Anderson also adds ½ teaspoon vinegar, but it's not traditional, so feel free to leave it out). You won't necessarily need all the sauce – it depends on how many aubergines you are doing, but when you've done it once, you'll want to do it again, so it won't go to waste. Grill that for 5 or 10 minutes until it is caramelised and bubbling. Don't burn your mouth.

We can't talk aubergines without mentioning baba ghanoush, an iconic aubergine dip from the Middle East. The key is live flame. It's usually done on a gas hob or (as Itamar Srulovich prefers) a charcoal grill. Get the outsides really black and the insides to the point of collapse (shut the door to the smoke alarm). Andi Oliver says you can start it off with a cook's blowtorch and then get them in the oven. Once they are tender, scoop out the insides, then for the traditional taste, add tahini, good olive oil, garlic and lemon. Andi adds a typical twist, banging in loads of roasted onions, garlic and oregano. Blitz it all up and job done.

Anna Jones builds on baba ghanoush with a mirza ghasemi. Browned garlic slices, turmeric, chopped fresh tomatoes, all cooked down, and then tomato purée and the same smoky barbecued aubergines you'd use for baba ghanoush. You can add chopped boiled eggs – she prefers it without. It's a lovely alternative, and the turmeric gives it a really rounded flavour.

If the idea of a spiced aubergine purée excites you, Nisha Katona says head to India. Aubergine is a brilliant substitute for the textures you often associate with meat and is one of India's most-loved vegetables. She does a dish called baingan bharta, which is not subtle, but is pretty amazing, served with rice or flatbread. Like baba ghanoush, you flame and soften your aubergines, and then add mustard oil, black salt, coriander and red onion. Big flavours. Black salt is a kiln-fired rock salt with a sulphurous, deep flavour – Nisha admits rotten eggs come to mind. But the dish is a humble one, intended to punch well above its weight in terms of flavour, and it does what it says on the tin.

'It's brutal, and aggressive, come on, come on. You don't need much.' – Nisha Katona

---

Panellist pick: ***Most aggravating food sounds***

Our audience voted the sound of chewing gum with your mouth open as their most annoying food-related sound.

Tim Hayward disputes the very idea. He says it is all cultural, and that he has no patience for being grumpy and prim around bodily functions and the noises they make. Many cultures actively value such sounds. A big belch at the end of a hearty meal? Bring it on, it's a proper appreciation.

Barry Smith offers a mitigating voice. Some people suffer from a condition called misophonia, a genuinely unpleasant reaction to triggering noises. But others spend hours scouring the web for videos of the soft sounds of people eating and cooking, trying to induce a feeling known as ASMR: autonomous sensory meridian response. It's the tingling feeling you get when listening to something really good. Frying bacon, for instance.

Barbecues

On the subject of brutal and aggressive, time for a topic still sometimes stuck in the past. Barbecuing still has a reputation for being a masculine style of cooking, whether because of tired tropes around big lumps of meat and making fire, or simply because it tends to be a leisure activity and, statistically, the everyday stuff still falls to women, while the fun stuff is more of an equal employer. But the TKC panel includes both Tim Hayward – a man with a gridiron tattooed on his arm – and Rachel McCormack, Queen of the Calçotadas, a Catalan onion feast food entirely centred on open flames. And both of them say barbecues should be about fun and friends and everyone pitching in while chilling out. Safe to say, we're pretty happy to leave the gender stereotyping in the 1970s, back where it belongs.

Be warned, as there are those who don't like a barbecue in any form. Barry Smith says the key reason barbecue smells (and tastes) so good is the heady mix of the Maillard reaction (from browning meat) and the specific compounds released when roasting meats on a barbecue. Compounds called pyrazines, pyridines and furans, among others, all combine to make most people's mouths water, but for others it is more of a pucker. The same people who dislike the smell of freshly brewed coffee usually have issues with barbecues since some of the same odour compounds are found in both.

I've been watching loads of TV shows about American BBQ, when it is all racks of ribs cooked for days. So, can the panel advise on what's best – low and slow or hot and fiery?

We've talked barbecue on a lot of shows. In Bristol, we talked to **Ray Lampe**, who goes by the name 'Dr BBQ', and was for a long time the head judge at the city's Grillstock Festival. He explained that the low-and-slow stuff is an American import, a set of techniques and flavours born in the Deep South. Typically, meat (and it nearly always is meat) is brined or dry-rubbed for flavour, and then cooked very slowly over smoke and fire. It's usually then finished with more rub, or a splash of sauce and a brief sizzle over a much hotter flame.

Tim Anderson says both American-style slow-cooking and the faster style of other culinary cultures have their appeal. Fast and furious? Go Korean with very thin cuts of meat, seared hot and therefore quick to cook. It gets rid of the risk of the British barbecue classic: black on the outside, bleeding in the middle.

For a low, slow, recipe, try using ox cheeks, which will take slow-cooking without drying out. Tim does them in a teriyaki-style sauce, cooked on a barbecue around the same temperature as you'd do them in an oven (most American barbecues have a lid). Don't be afraid to use cast-iron cookware on the barbecue, to braise the cheeks slowly in a sauce. A foil tray works as well. Do keep them covered (in foil or butcher's paper) for most of the cooking time (allow at least 6 hours), to keep the juices in. The idea is to infuse the smoky flavour into the meat and get a bit of outside char and extra flavour. Think of your barbecue as a heat source, oven, grill and hob all in one: it's controllable, and versatile. You don't have to use the hottest of heats and just blacken everything.

How about a lamb joint? Andi Oliver makes a sauce from sweated down onions, garlic and chilli, plus tamarind, chipotle, brown sugar and red wine. Simmer it down until thick. Then you want a butterflied leg of lamb, which you start off on the fire with just a dry rub (salt, chilli, paprika, garlic and cumin will work – this is a big flavour sauce so subtle flavours will get lost). Once you get some nice colour on it, start painting it with your sauce and keep the joint moving. Move it to cooler areas to get it cooked through, and hotter ones to colour it up once it's done. In other words, buy yourself a digital probe.

If you don't have a lid or 6 hours to spare, Nisha Katona advises that you can use a similar technique for fast cooking. She does mackerel spread with a sauce of English mustard paste, lemon juice, salt and coriander leaf. Just wrap the fish in foil and put it on the barbecue for about 8–10 minutes. It's great with a mango roasted in foil until it liquefies – just drizzle it over the fish.

I need some good vegetarian options for the barbecue. Please not halloumi – it's all I get offered and I'm so fed up with it!

Rachel McCormack says you'll struggle to get the right onions for a Catalan calçotada in the UK, but you can replicate it with leeks. You have to get them touching the flame, properly burning the outside. And then you wrap them in newspaper and leave them for 10–15 minutes to steam through. When you eat it, you pull the burnt bit off and dip the rest in romesco sauce, which is just roasted tomato and garlic, hazelnuts, almonds, olive oil and vinegar, plus unsmoked paprika. It's the solution to many things, but certainly to making vegetables the equal of any meat dish. Try it with cabbage as well.

Andi Oliver opts for corn-on-the-cob. Good with romesco, of course, but also with a flavoured butter, and a bit of feta crumbled on top. And Anna Jones says try twisting a salad. Barbecued lettuce – something like a baby gem or a cos – can be put straight on the grilling rack, charred a bit, and then chopped and made into a simple Caesar salad. Just add croutons (which you can also toast on the barbecue), Parmesan and a bit of dressing. From plain to punchy in a few flaming steps.

Don't forget as well, that a barbecue can be used as a big outdoor hob. Rachel McCormack points out you don't have to think in terms of 'Things with Sauce on a Fire'. What about a paella? Meaty or veggie, easy to do, and always a crowd-pleaser.

Top tip: *Stop putting your tomatoes in the fridge*

Unthinkingly shoving your tomatoes in the fridge? Stop right now, says Peter Barham. Tomatoes are a brilliant source of umami. But tomatoes on their own have no flavour. It's only generated when you cut the tomato, at which point an enzyme in the liquid reacts with the fleshy part of the fruit. (And yes, he has experimented with syringes and extractions of each bit of the thing to find out.) The enzyme is destroyed if the temperature gets below 4°C, 'So you should never ever, ever, ever put tomatoes in the fridge.' Got it?

And finally ... we asked our audience on the Isle of Wight about their most traumatising food experience.

We couldn't help wincing with one dutiful granddaughter who went to visit her 'Mad Granny up North'. Eating breakfast one morning, she suggested the milk was off. Absolutely not, apparently. Mad Granny made her finish the entire bowl of cereal. It was only afterwards our hero realised the milk was in fact ... fish stock for that night's pie.

厨柜
SOY

September

Excuses to eat this month include:

Meatopia, London (pretty much what you'd imagine)

Egremont Crab Fair (apples, not shellfish, with bonus points for the World Gurning Championships)

Sweetcorn Fayre, Isle of Wight (all thyngs ynvolvyng corn)

Manchester Food and Drink Festival

Ludlow Food Festival (castles and cake)

Aldeburgh Food Festival (music, salt spray and excellent fish and chips)

Rosh Hashanah (Jewish New Year, apples and honey)

Michaelmas (as in goose, rent, gifts and an excuse for a fair)

The moon this month is made of **raclette**

Raclette is both a dish and a couple of cheeses. The dish is melted cheese, and the cheeses, one from the Swiss Valois and one from French Savoie, are perfect for melting, usually with an open flame or grill. They are washed-rind cheeses, pressed and just a little bit boingy when eaten unmelted. Somerset Ogleshield is a milder English alternative, excellent on potatoes, in cheeseburgers or on toast. Autumn is a-coming in, and crispy, stringy, melty cheese is here to help us ease into it.

This month *The Kitchen Cabinet* is in **Manchester**, known as Cottonopolis to the Victorians. It's famed for its offally nice black pudding and triperies, and home to the second-largest Chinatown in the UK.

Key flavours for September include **apples** and **cauliflower**, **game** and **grapes**. It's wine harvest time in Europe, hoorah!

And we are also thinking about:

- The best way to make a fish-finger sandwich
- Matching whisky with wasabi
- Red wine-spill disasters

- The best material for spoons
- And a superlative Scotch egg

Welcome to Manchester, once called Warehouse City, and the heart of the UK's nineteenth-century textile industry. Today you can tour the sites of many a mill-worker's meal, before choosing between old-style English tripe with vinegar and something decidedly more modern. We've been to Manchester twice, enjoying the gadgetry of the Science and Industry Museum, as well as giving the TKC thumbs up to the modernist glories of the Toast Rack in Fallowfield. We've wandered the streets of Manchester's Chinatown, too, admiring the Ming Dynasty Arch before breaking off for bao buns and noodles.

Top tip: *Red wine spills*

Prof. Barry Smith says there is no truth to the idea that white wine will get out red wine stains. It's based on a vague bit of science, which explains why lemon juice works: the acid breaks up the pigmentation that stays and stains. But white wine won't. He says one of his favourite memories as a student was watching a fellow student waiter spill a tiny bit of red wine on a very expensively besuited man in a Glaswegian restaurant. 'This suit cost me £600, but I'll take £300,' said he. Quick as a flash, she answered that she'd get it out, and sloshed a glass of white wine on him. It didn't work (obviously) but he had to spend the rest of the meal gently dripping.

Chinese food in the UK and the greatness of soy sauce

Chinese restaurants and takeaways are the mainstay of many a British high street. We've enthusiastically adopted Chinese ingredients and techniques, but, as with so many cuisines, most of us know Chinese food mainly as an Anglicised hybrid. But Manchester is one of a number of cities in the UK to have a significant Chinese population and a recognised Chinatown, where it's possible to sample the rich variety of regional traditions, as well as buy ingredients to recreate certain dishes at home.

Where does our love of Chinese food come from? It's been a slow burner. There have been small Chinese communities in the UK since the mid-nineteenth century. The first Chinese restaurants catered for these communities, along with the very occasional westerner venturing forth in a spirit of adventure. In 1884, the Great Health Exhibition in London introduced a slightly wider public to certain dishes – Queen Victoria had the Chinese cooks from the exhibition brought to Windsor to cook her birds' nest soup. By the early twentieth century, a couple of London restaurants – The Cathay and Maxims – had opened, aiming at a western audience, and proved very popular.

It was around then that the first significant numbers of Chinese settled in Manchester. The community grew slowly over the next few decades, and then boomed in the 1940s and 1950s. We spoke to writer and Chinese culinary expert Deh-ta Hsiung, who came to the UK in 1949, and remembered having to travel miles to find good Chinese food. He told us that the pivotal era was the 1950s, when Britain recognised the new government in Beijing, and many of the diplomats who had represented the previous regime found themselves out of work. Many stayed, and opened restaurants.

I'm like a rabbit in headlights in a Chinese restaurant. I go in determined to be different, then panic and order the same old stuff. What are the panel's go-to dishes?

Lizzie Mabbott grew up in Hong Kong and says her early memories of Chinese food in the UK were mainly of surprise. There was chop suey, an entirely made-up dish that was pure Anglo-Chinese (or American-Chinese, depending on the version of the invention myth you read); fried rice, which is a leftover dish rarely served formally in China; and then a whole range of sweet-and-sour meat, often with pineapple. Many of the early restaurants were Cantonese, and Cantonese food became synonymous with Chinese food for a while.

Lizzie's heritage is Cantonese, and her advice is to order a roasted meat – either duck or char sui, which is roasted pork. Get it on the bone for more flavour and a lot more fun.

Tim Hayward agrees that a lot of what the British call Chinese food wouldn't be recognised in China. But he doesn't see it as a thing to be ashamed of. Culinary culture is adapted by its practitioners, changing to suit the local taste and ingredients. But you can enjoy both.

His favourite Chinese restaurant is Sichuan, and he enjoys it both for the fantastic flavour combinations and the menu translations. 'Strange taste fragrant rabbit' is gorgeous, but his absolute go-to is the 'fire exploded kidneys', which he describes as the most delicious thing ever. Don't be afraid to choose just because you like the sound of something.

Sichuan is also the route Tim Anderson takes. He suggests trying mapo tofu, which is, as you'd imagine, primarily tofu, with meat used almost as a garnish. It's very, very spicy, with a moreish heat from the Sichuan peppercorns, and it slips down beautifully.

If you aren't sure of your heat tolerance, or you just fancy something stunning, Jeremy Pang says there's no need to pick just one dish. Go for dim sum instead. Nobody is quite sure where it comes from, but various stories suggest it sprang from tea houses, which did not traditionally serve food. It's said that one old lady felt a bit sorry for her customers, who were very hungry, so she went into her kitchen, made what she could from her ingredients, and fed them dumplings. And then her neighbours got competitive and made more intricate dumplings for their own customers, and it snowballed from there. If you're in Hong Kong, you'll find the dim sum places full at 5am, with elderly customers having a great time – plus it tends to be half price.

Soy sauces: how are they different, and what do I use them all for?

One of the most characteristic ingredients of Chinese cookery is soy sauce. Jeremy Pang says the wealth of different types can be a source of some confusion. Think of soy sauce as fine wine. When you swirl it round a glass, you get the classic 'legs' as it sticks to the sides. The more leggy, the higher the sugar content. With soy sauce, the dark soys have a higher sugar to salt content, so they are more caramelised in texture. That makes them better for colour and stickiness, so ideal for slow-cooked, slow-braised, caramelised dishes, like dong po rou (braised pork belly). Light soy is saltier, so good for seasoning meats, fish and vegetables, or pouring into a fried rice dish to give you the saltiness you need.

Then there's Japanese soy. Jeremy says the big difference there is that Japanese soy sauce doesn't have added sugar during the fermentation process. It's different to Chinese sauces and works brilliantly as a dip. Tim Anderson tends to buy an unpasteurised Japanese soy sauce, which he says has more complexity and freshness than a lot of the more generic sauces.

Tim's advice is to always check the ingredients. A lot of supermarket soy sauces aren't really soy sauce at all. They're basically brown water with salt, MSG and some kind of acid. Not brewed or fermented in any way, just sets of liquid flavourings. So read the bottle and buy the ones that list water, soya beans and salt and not a lot else. (Japanese sauces and some Chinese ones also use wheat; Chinese versions use sugar or molasses.)

Panellist pick: ***The best possible Scotch egg***

Rob Owen-Brown makes a Manchester egg. He invented it with a group of similarly minded Scotch egg aficionados one night in a Manchester pub (The Castle: it should probably have a blue plaque), and it is the ultimate pub snack. It's a pickled egg, wrapped in 60% black pudding, 40% pork sausagemeat. He usually coats it in panko breadcrumbs, plus smoked paprika and English mustard powder. But there's more. It was originally rolled in salt and vinegar crisps ... Cynical? Try a quick version – next time you are in a pub, take a pickled egg and a packet of salt and vinegar crisps, crush them up, and roll the egg around in it.

Top tip: ***Wasabi and whisky (no, really)***

Barry Smith has a neat trick with which to wow your dinner guests and work your way through your surplus whisky (apparently it happens). Whisky is an aggressive beast and tends to set your mouth on fire. But have a handful of wasabi nuts on hand. They're very spicy and will give you a trigeminal burn in your mouth. While it's still on fire, try your whisky. Your brain will have been hit with fire already, so when the whisky goes in, it strips off the fieriness, leaving you with the pure flavour of the drink, not just the burn of the booze.

Noodles

The British have dumplings, the Italians have pasta and the Chinese have noodles. We first encountered TKC regular Jeremy Pang on an episode we recorded in London's Chinatown, where he gave us a running commentary of a noodle-making demonstration by chef Kam Po, former executive chef at Ken Lo's Memories of China in Belgravia. We watched open-mouthed as he took a basic dough of wheat flour, water, salt and a little oil, and then gave it hell.

The first stage is to beat the dough repeatedly on a table until it is elastic enough to work with (it got a little noisy). Then comes the twist or plait, a sort of repeated figure of eight done with the hands, swapping hands each time to make it balanced. You end up with a long, even twist. This is cut into sections. The dough is now at the threading point: the next bit is one of the nearest things to magic we've witnessed while making the show. Each short length of dough is gently, firmly, pulled into noodles using a rhythmic, hypnotic, flicking and pulling motion, in which dough is slowly stretched, folded, stretched and folded until the wizard/noodlemaker is holding an incredibly long set of noodles. Each strand is perfect (and not sticking to another one). We had to pause the show briefly for a heartfelt round of applause.

What are the panel's favourite ways to make noodles the star of the show, not just an afterthought when you forgot to cook any rice?

First up, a warning: the length of noodles is deeply symbolic across East Asia. So don't hack them up or you'll suffer short marriages and short lives.

Sophie Wright suggests a salad. After all, it's still pretty warm outside, so we should make the most of it. She uses rice noodles for this. Cook them briefly and rinse well in cold water so that they don't stick together – you need to get rid of all the starch, so don't scrimp on this stage or you'll get a solid lump. You can also throw the cooked noodles into a bowl of cold water and leave.

Spicy noodle salad

You can make this with leftover noodles or cook them up specially. All you need do is make a punchy peanut sauce: just minced lemongrass, chilli, fish sauce, lime and loads of holy basil. Then you need your noodles and lots of vegetables. Again, you can use them fresh, raw, just cooked through or you can also use leftover vegetables – whatever you have to hand. Toss all of this with the noodles and it's a really easy and quick supper.

Another cold noodle dish is the Korean naengmyeon. It originated in North Korea as Pyongyang naengmyeon, before being brought South by people fleeing the war. Jordan Bourke says there are different versions in the two countries – South Korean recipes tend to rely on a beef broth, while in North Korea venison is also used. The noodles are normally made from buckwheat, a bit like the Japanese soba noodles, and they are mixed into the broth along with a range of toppings, usually including an egg, plus some mustard oil and vinegar.

We talked a bit about Korean food when we visited New Malden and met **Nicole Cho** of Jin Go Gae restaurant. She brought us her version of naengmyeon, which balanced the buckwheat noodles with cucumber, gochugaru chilli power, Korean pear and a soft-boiled egg on top. She explained that it was particularly good when having a Korean barbecue, when the chilled soup provides a real contrast to the warm charcoal-grilled meat.

If you prefer hot noodles, Jordan recommends chap chae, based on a potato starch noodle called dangmyun, though you could use another noodle if you have a preference. You just cook them, then soak in soy sauce, toasted sesame oil and then combine them with fried vegetables.

Andi Oliver, meanwhile, uses cooked flat egg noodles mixed with eggs, cream cheese, cottage cheese, maybe some sour cream, vanilla, sultanas and a bit of sugar to make lokshen, a Jewish pudding that is definitely not on the light summer meal side. Just combine the ingredients, let them sit overnight, and bake it. It's particularly good served for breakfast with a bit of plum compote.

Tim Anderson wants you to make ramen. Ramen should use quite specialist noodles, made with added alkaline salts (kansui), which strengthen the gluten structure in the noodles, giving them a characteristic springy bite. Ramen can be as simple or as complicated as you want, but noodles are a key element and it is definitely a dish to show them at their best. Tim also has another way to make noodles the star. He holds the TKC record for eating the fastest-moving noodles. It's a Japanese method of noodle eating called *nagashi sōmen*. You sit at a table that has a bamboo shoot propped up running along it, with a tap or hose at one end, making a stream down the shoot. The chef then drops in bunches of cooked noodles and you have to reach in and pluck them out with chopsticks, dipping them in sauces and eating before they go rushing by.

I've got a massive stash of instant noodle packets, the little ones in plastic bags with flavour sachets. Beyond the obvious stuff it says on the packet, what else can I do to use them up?

Both Tim Anderson and Jordan Bourke agree that you shouldn't think of instant noodles as a dirty secret to be used up on the sly. Fresh noodles are great, but there's certainly scope for dried varieties too.

Jordan is fond of a Korean technique called *ppu-syeo-ppu-syeo*, which translates as 'destroy, destroy'. You just have to hammer the noodles in the packet until they are broken up, and then use the spice sachet to flavour them. When you open them up, you have noodle crisps, easy and enjoyable eaten straight from the packet.

Uncooked instant noodles are, indeed, great, agrees Tim Anderson. He pulverises them and uses them for texture and flavour in the same way you might use breadcrumbs or crushed pretzels. Try running them through pork mince to pimp your sausagemeat, and then – even better – use that sausagemeat to make a Scotch egg. You can add more noodle powder, along with the seasoning sachets, to the coating.

Science: ***Best material for spoons***

Dr Zoe Laughlin is working on making the best spoon in the world. She's been experimenting with blindfolded volunteers eating various things from various spoons made from different materials. Shape plays a role too – ideally we would all have spoons made to fit our exact mouth shapes. But the material does manifestly change the taste of foods. Try eating tomato from a copper spoon – the acid reacts and it is properly unpleasant. Even a stainless-steel spoon – the most common metal for cutlery – affects the flavour of your food. So, if you want the ultimate meal, with the best possible taste, what should you choose? Simple. Just go for gold. Or gold-plated.

Offal

Manchester sits at the heart of a region rich in local delicacies. Along with a wealth of imported cuisines, you can still bury yourself in black pudding, pasty barm or parched peas, all foods which serve as a reminder of the city's industrial past. These are the foods that fuelled the Industrial Revolution in the city, and are, as you'd expect, hearty fodder for working people. But while we never say no to pastry, and are always prepared for a dried pulse, we couldn't come to Manchester without talking about something currently heading for extinction. Time, we feel, to talk tripe.

We recently had some visitors who told us they didn't eat tripe. We weren't actually considering serving it, but now they've said it, I sort of want to. Can the panel convince me to convert them (and myself)?

In the 1960s, Manchester was home to around 260 tripe shops. Dr Annie Gray says it was pretty popular. It had a long history, not as something gross, but as a high-class food. After all, it was meat, and meat was expensive – most people in the past could rarely afford any meat, and the idea that you'd refuse something just because it was strong tasting or a bit of a challenge to cook was ludicrous. If anything, time and effort made it more interesting, as it was a good way to show off the skills of the cooks you employed. That changed during the Industrial Revolution, when it became, not cheap, but more of a working-class food. It was a good, fast alternative to other street foods like fish and chips because you could buy it ready-processed and eat it as is or cook it up for a quick supper after a long shift. It was very, very nutritious.

Tim Hayward is a huge fan. He explains that there are four types of tripe, from each of the cow's four stomachs. Grass is not an easy thing to digest, so cows have evolved a system whereby they chew grass, partially digest it, belch it back up again, chew, digest and repeat. Slowly the grass moves through the stomach system, enabling them to get out all the goodness they need. The process is called rumination, hence cows (and some other animals) are called ruminants. In a cow you've got stomachs called the rumen, the reticulum, the omasum and the abomasum, producing, in order, blanket or flat tripe, honeycomb tripe, book tripe and reed tripe. Honeycomb is usually regarded as the best. Tripe needs to be processed professionally, which involves cleaning, scraping and bleaching. It's a very skilled process.

Once you've got your tripe, you can do all sorts with it. The English classics are tripe and onions, or tripe just dressed with vinegar, but as Rachel McCormack points out, they can be pretty rubbery. Sophie Wright says there are better classics from the continent: try it Spanish style poached in a rich tomato sauce with plenty of garlic, sweated off onions, spicy chorizo, tinned tomatoes, white wine, sherry vinegar and add some cannellini beans to finish.

Tim Hayward would like you to take a trip to Florence to eat lampredotto from the market there. It's made with reed tripe, slow-cooked and sliced. Tim describes buying it from a huge guy with a broken nose and a massive knife, who may query whether you mean it when you order the tripe. But insist. He'll whip off a slice or two, ask you which sauce you want, red or green (it doesn't matter, as they are both incredibly hot), and serve you a tripe sandwich that is one of the most stupendous things you'll ever eat. It tastes like all the bits in a roast that you carefully secrete away and scoff in the kitchen when nobody is watching.

Local chef **James Taylor** brought us something from the other end of the scale. He makes KFT, or Kentucky fried tripe, which is exactly what you'd imagine. As ever, there's little that can't be improved by deep-fat frying. Tim Anderson agrees that this is transformative but says you can also griddle it. He says he was converted by a tripe taco from a truck in Los Angeles. It had been slow-cooked with spices and orange, until it was beautifully tender. Then it was crisped on a very hot griddle and served in a taco with a chilli and tomato salsa, fresh radish and lime.

I'm a bit bored with just devilling my kidneys and hearts. Any ideas to jazz them up?

Nisha Katona says once you get over the alarm the words 'gizzard and hearts' bring, you could try cooking them Asian style. You can get gizzards very easily at Asian butchers, and while they are chewy, that's something valued in a lot of eastern cookery. Soft meat is for lightweights. She does a slowly cooked spiced stew with onion, ginger, garlic, all sweated off, and then the gizzards and hearts (chicken or duck) added in. Spice it with heaps of good garam masala, turmeric and chilli; fry it all for a few minutes to brown, and then add half a tin of chopped tomatoes. Finally, add some dried plums for a bit of sweetness, plus salt, plenty of fresh green chilli and a touch of brown sugar. Top that up with water and leave it to simmer very gently for a couple of hours until the gizzards are tender.

Itamar Srulovich agrees that spice is nice. He likes to flash-fry offal, be it kidneys or heart or liver, and just serve it with salt and pepper. But you can oomph it up with a bit of lemon and garlic, or cumin is great with liver. And if you have a fryer, deep-fried breaded liver strips with cumin are, while a little bit dirty, quite delicious.

If you're not sure about offal and this isn't converting you, Andi Oliver offers an entry-level idea: sweetbreads. The thymus gland of (usually) veal, they do need a bit of preparation, deveining and skinning, but if you roll them in smoked paprika, flour and garlic powder, deep-fry them and serve with creamed sweetcorn, plus a bit of parsley and garlic, she promises they will be lovely.

Top tip: *Fish-finger sandwiches*

It has to be fast, says Zoe Laughlin. White bread, a good layer of butter, plus ketchup, which will melt to form a sauce, and then grilled fish fingers. Rob-Owen Brown might quibble (he really did), saying a deep-fat fryer was vital, but in the fast fish-finger world, a grill is quicker. Get it done, get it grilled, get it on your plate.

Apples

As we slowly move towards autumn, we bid a sad farewell to the soft fruits of summer. But in their place come other tantalising tastes, including the staple of many a lunchbox, often taken for granted, but worthy of so much more: the humble apple.

Apples are everywhere, but if we only shop at supermarkets our choice is strictly limited. We've eaten apples all over the country, but one of our favourite places to perambulate in search of the perfect fruit is Brogdale, down in Kent. It's been the home of the National Fruit Collection since 1954 and counts around 2200 varieties of apples among its orchards. We spoke to **Mike Austin**, one of the guides at Brogdale, who urged us to get out and experiment with apple types. How about a striped beefing, once used to make Norfolk biffins, a Victorian street snack made by drying out the apples until they were shrivelled, soft and beautifully sweet? Or a knobby russet, which has an extra chromosome and is spectacularly ugly, but also delicious?

Heritage varieties don't always look very nice, or yield reliably, so they don't make it to the supermarkets. But they often have a fantastic flavour.

Barry Smith says another issue with apples is how people often keep them. They really aren't great stored in a fruit bowl. When ripening fruits like apples, which are climacteric (i.e. they ripen after being picked), they give off a little gas when ripening.

That then gives off ethylene, which is one of the triggers to make other fruit start to ripen too. In this way, a ripe apple will trigger a chain reaction. It's one of the reasons why for longer-term storage, you need to keep them cool and not in contact with each other. In a mixed fruit bowl, your apples will be spared while other fruits are sacrificed. If you put apples and bananas in the same bowl, your apples will merrily give off their gases, and speed up the ripening process in the bananas. And nobody wants black bananas.

Barry says that understanding the processes at work in ripening apples helps us to use them better. They are picked as mature fruit but giving them time to fully ripen allows the starches to break down to make sugars, increasing the sweetness and improving the flavour. A lot of the flavour (and goodness) is stored just under the skin, in compounds called antioxidants. They're needed by the apple to heal the skin if it gets punctured, but they also contain a lot of the flavour (and goodness). So don't peel your apples.

And if you do get browning on a bit of cut flesh? Embrace it. The phenolic compound that is created by the process of browning is really good at combining with the sulpher-y elements in garlic and onion to turn them into new, odourless molecules. So, getting your teeth round a browned apple is a great way to stop your breath (or fingers) smelling of allium.

My partner is a fruit grower, so we always have a lot of apples about. Can the panel help me out with some showstopping dishes, beyond the usual run of jams, jellies, pies and crumbles?

Eating apples is great but cooking with them can be even greater. Angela Harnett does a sort of apple pommes dauphinoise, using peeled, thinly sliced apples, all pressed into a ring or tin and cooked very, very slowly. It's like the best bit of a tarte tatin. Tim Anderson agrees that tatin-like things are a great idea. They're simple, but easy to pimp. You always start with a caramel, before adding sliced or quartered apples, and then the puff pastry top. But you can add anything into your caramel. Miso works – but the best he's done was with malt syrup and bourbon in the caramel.

Annie Gray points out that the division into cookers and eaters is relatively recent and unique to the UK. Older recipes are really worth trying, but don't use cooking apples for anything that doesn't specify a Bramley – a nice dual-purpose or all-rounder like a Cox or a Braeburn or a Russet works well though. She likes making apple cheese, a staple of the late eighteenth and nineteenth centuries. It's essentially a moulded marmalade, but it's vegetarian friendly, and tastes fab.

Apple cheese

You need about a kilo of peeled, cored apples, chopped roughly, plus half a kilo of sugar and the peel and juice of a couple of lemons. Boil the apples in 250ml of water until they are soft, then add the sugar, peel and juice and boil it really hard, mashing up the apples, until it goes brown and, according to nineteenth-century food writer Eliza Acton, 'leaves the bottom of the pan visibly dry.' You can then pour it into a buttered ceramic mould and leave it to set overnight. When you want to serve it, the secret is to stick slivered almonds all over it (Jay said it looked like a stegosaurus). It would have been served with custard, but Annie says it is brilliant with cheese or, even better, Parmesan ice cream, another of her favourite eighteenth-century recipes (see page 173).

Sophie Wright is also a fan of apples and cheese. She suggests taking something that seems like the usual kind of thing and giving it a twist. A really good apple pie, served with a hunk of sharp cheese, for example. We talked about apple pie and cheese on one of our lockdown shows, and loads of listeners contacted us in praise of the combination. Barry Smith says add something into your apple pie to enhance the cheese. Garam masala and vanilla extract work well. Or, says Tim Anderson, try red miso in the apple – and serve the cheese layered on top of the pie. If you are really going for it, choose a cheese that crisps up well, and bake the cheese not just into the pie, but browned and bubbling on top.

Margins are useful, but here's a bigger blank space to make September your own.

And finally, we asked our audience in Lambeth to tell us about their kitchen gadget nightmares.

We can't help but be awed by the man whose friend-of-a-friend (apparently) said he was never, ever making mash again. Turned out he was making gloriously fine ricer-style mash … in a garlic press.

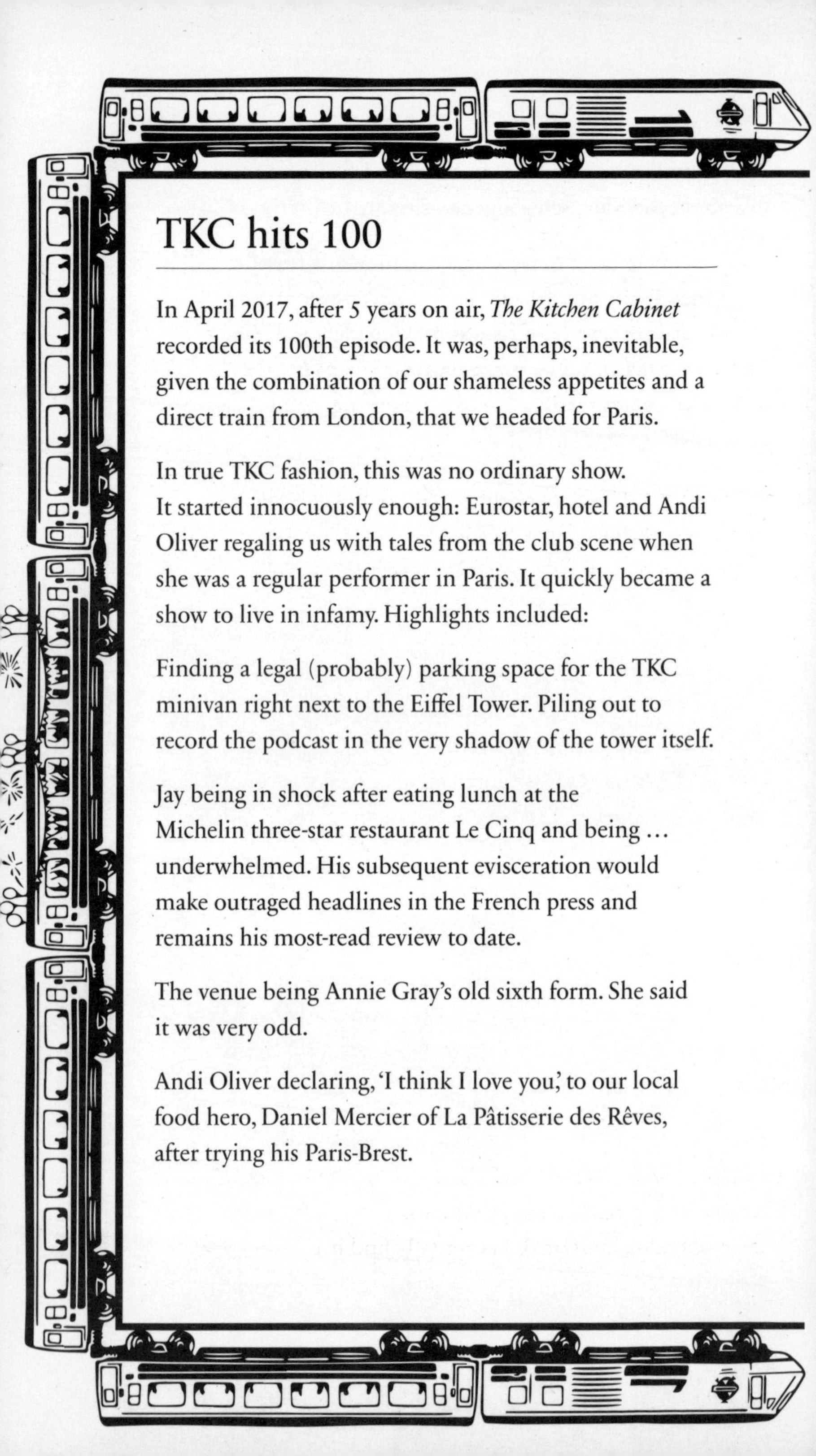

TKC hits 100

In April 2017, after 5 years on air, *The Kitchen Cabinet* recorded its 100th episode. It was, perhaps, inevitable, given the combination of our shameless appetites and a direct train from London, that we headed for Paris.

In true TKC fashion, this was no ordinary show. It started innocuously enough: Eurostar, hotel and Andi Oliver regaling us with tales from the club scene when she was a regular performer in Paris. It quickly became a show to live in infamy. Highlights included:

Finding a legal (probably) parking space for the TKC minivan right next to the Eiffel Tower. Piling out to record the podcast in the very shadow of the tower itself.

Jay being in shock after eating lunch at the Michelin three-star restaurant Le Cinq and being … underwhelmed. His subsequent evisceration would make outraged headlines in the French press and remains his most-read review to date.

The venue being Annie Gray's old sixth form. She said it was very odd.

Andi Oliver declaring, 'I think I love you,' to our local food hero, Daniel Mercier of La Pâtisserie des Rêves, after trying his Paris-Brest.

Daniel bringing enough pâtisserie for the full audience of 300 people. Since closed, at the time La Pâtisserie des Rêves was iconic and it's fair to say our audience's attention was a little divided once they realised what was in all those beribboned boxes on the stage.

The drive back from the venue along the banks of the Seine into central Paris, all of us high on sugar and excited to have a night in Paris.

The brasserie where we ate providing so much food it defeated even us. There was the Dover sole in a salty, sticky pool of glorious browned butter (one of them lost its tail on serving – another appeared as if by magic). There was the andouillette and chips. There were rillettes and gherkins and baskets of crusty baguette. There was cheese. And then there were desserts – prunes in Armagnac, crème brûlée – all the classics. We were gravely assured all would go to waste if we did not eat them, and we did our absolute best.

The walk back to the hotel – a futile attempt to digest.

Turns out you can have a food hangover.

Tim Anderson getting up early to go on a ramen crawl (how, after all the andouillette?). He sent pictures to the rest of us from every stop. Paris, he says, has some of the best ramen outside Japan.

Sudden alarm from producer Laurence who had mislaid the minivan, parked carefully the night before in an overly generic underground car park somewhere near where we ate. (He did eventually find it.)

Half of the production team heading to Versailles. More pictures, this time of the palace seen sideways from a wildly careening golf buggy. They said they felt a bit sick.

The other half of the production team and the remains of the panel walking dazedly along the Canal St Martin in search of the ability to eat anything ever again.

Discovering canelé. Recovering the ability to eat. Buying more canelé for the train home.

Paris, we agreed, would be hard to top. What would we do for our 200th episode? New York? Las Vegas (not exactly food heaven, but it also has an Eiffel Tower)?

Episode 200 fell in January 2021 … we recorded it remotely in our bedrooms, surrounded by duvets to muffle the echo. But it's true what they say. We'll always have Paris.

WEST WING

October

Spooky and other dates for this month's food diary:

Goatober (a great excuse to try a popular meat)

The British Cheese Awards (at the Royal Bath & West Dairy Show, what's not to like?)

The Golden Spurtle (porridge, bagpipes, mad skills)

Falmouth Oyster Festival
(and start of prime oyster season)

Apple Day (eating and identification of your mystery tree)

Diwali (the Hindu festival of lights and a great excuse for sticky sweets)

Punkie Night (West Country, involves hollowed-out mangelwurzels, which is harder to do than it sounds)

Hallowe'en (soul cakes and trick or treat sugar rush)

The moon this month is made of **Vacherin**

In season from September to May, there are two types of Vacherin: the PDO raw milk Vacherin du Haut-Doubs, and the more mass-market pasteurised Vacherin Mont d'Or (confusingly, the Haut-Doubs one is called Mont d'Or as well, so look for the Haut-Doubs bit on the box). The top looks like a snow-covered landscape of hills and valleys. It's an autumn cheese par excellence, served ripe and raw with a spoon and some bread, or baked until crusty and gooey and eaten as a hearty, soupy dip. Good ones are pricey, but they are worth it.

This month *The Kitchen Cabinet* is in **Leicester**, in the Midlands, known for its space centre and its spice-filled Golden Mile.

Key flavours this month are **quince**, **cobnuts**, **squash** and the start of the new **shellfish season**.

And we are also thinking about:

- Whether to prick our sausages
- Synergistic umami
- The best box sets and food to eat while watching

- Marmite and music
- And why you should never put your eggs in the fridge

Welcome to Leicester, a vibrant city at the heart of an area known for wide-open fields, huge skies and a lot of vegetable growers. Europe's biggest covered market is quite the draw, selling produce both local and from further afield. As with so many visitors, we came for the curry, and stayed to visit the National Space Centre, because who doesn't love a great big rocket? In between reaching for the stars, we nibbled on Diwali sweet treats as well as salty snacks, for Leicester is also the home to the factory that produces nearly all of the UK's Bombay mix, as well as the biggest crisp factory in the world.

Sweets

October sees the start of Diwali, celebrated globally by Hindus, as well as Sikhs and Jains. Leicester has the biggest Diwali outside India, and for 5 days the city is alight with candles and oil lamps, while its many bakeries and restaurants glitter with the sparkle of sugar. Local restaurateur **Dharmesh Lakhani** of Bobby's Restaurant on Leicester's Golden Mile says it's a brilliant time to be in the city, with an electric atmosphere in the restaurant, and huge crowds celebrating in the street. Expect fireworks and stage shows, and a big emphasis on sweets intended for giving and receiving in an outburst of joy.

Dharmesh brought some of the most popular ones with him. First up were ghugra, a crescent-shaped pastry with a filling of semolina, almonds and pistachios (they didn't last long when they reached the panel). Then there were barfi, a classic Indian sweet made from condensed milk richly flavoured with fruit, which come in a wide range of different forms, some with nuts, some chocolate-dipped, some with candied fruit. We also ate kaju katli, which are cashew-filled diamonds covered with silver-gilt.

Dr Zoe Laughlin cautions that, unlike gold, which is inert, silver does have a flavour. It's totally safe to eat, but if you want a bit of fun, try coating a plain-ish biscuit with gold and another with silver and see which one you prefer. Silver should give you a sort of bitter fizz, but that can be an asset that you can use in your cooking.

'Silver is more than just bling on your biscuit – it bounces off the sweetness and pairs nicely with the taste.' – Zoe Laughlin

Sumayya Usmani says sweets of this type are a big part of Pakistani heritage too. Mithai (the term just means 'sweetmeats') are not only beautiful, but appeal to the almost universal Pakistani sweet tooth. We tried the Pakistani mithai when we went to Bradford. **Hur Ahmed**, from Nafees Bakers & Sweets, explained that when the bakery first opened, the recipes were all supplied by the owner's father, still living in Pakistan. He'd record them onto tape cassettes and send them over. This included laddu, made with gram (chickpea) flour and pumpkin seeds; gulab jamun, the rose syrup-imbibed sponges very popular as dessert in 'Indian' restaurants, and jalebi, which are deep-fried before being soaked in sugar syrup. And yes, the panel was a bit high on the sugar after this.

Sugary sweets are part of the British celebratory tradition as well. Rob Owen-Brown has quite a line in party favours, ranging from chocolate mousetraps with little white mice in (nothing says nuptials like a decapitated mouse) to giant Parma Violets, intended to be used as plates. They used, he said, a lot of purple food colouring, which does have the effect of going straight through you. How many wedding caterers have had to have reassuring conversations with their clients the next day about how their bowels are just fine really, just chalk it up to the edible crockery?

Sweets are particularly festive feeling at fairs or while we're on holiday – think candy floss, seaside rock and toffee apples. When we went to Nottingham we met **Ray Whitehead**, who'd been making and selling sugar confectionery at the city's Goose Fair for over 60 years. His grandfather had started the business, selling a speciality known as a cock on a stick. It's a pulled sugar cockerel. On a stick. And it is very difficult to do because pulling sugar is hot, sticky, dangerous work, which is time-critical and very fiddly. Ray has trained many, many people in the skill of making cocks, but he says it's quite an art form. And in Nottingham, people are particular. You can only show a cock if it has a good shape.

What are the easiest sweets to make at home?

Jocky Petrie suggests stained-glass shards. Easy to make with kids, fun by themselves, but also pretty snazzy as a garnish for cheesecakes or other desserts when you want to add a bit of a wow.

Stained-glass sweets

All you need are boiled sweets in different colours. Take them out of the wrappers (you'd be surprised) and lay them out on a baking sheet, close, but not touching (a silicone mat is helpful here). Place it in a low oven, at about 100°C, and wait until the sweets melt and run into each other, forming a multicoloured flat sheet of flavoured sugar. Cool, and simply snap into shards.

Pâte de fruit

Sophie Wright says pâte de fruit is fun. Take 500g raspberries (or similar fruit), 500g sugar, boiled to soft ball, which is about 112°C, and feel free to add a bit of pectin to help it set (you're effectively making boingy jam). Set it in a tray and cut it into squares when it is cool. For a final flourish, roll the squares in caster sugar.

Rob Owen-Brown goes for toffee. Recipes vary, but the secret is in the sugar. Most toffees start with simply boiling sugar, so cooking toffee means mastering the stages of sugar boiling. If you've got a digital thermometer, it's a bit easier, but you can also test the stages by taking a little bit of your mixture and dropping it into a bowl of cold water and then feeling the texture. Once your sugar reaches the desired temperature, that's when you add the other ingredients – it is the sugar that will give them the consistency you want. So, for a soft, chewy toffee, aim for 110–120°C or soft ball (it'll feel squidgy between your fingers if you are using the cold water test). For a harder toffee, go for 146–154°C, aka hard crack.

After that, it's all about the additions. How about butterscotch? Take your sugar to hard crack, then add some double cream and a lump of butter – use a really big pan, though, for it will foam up massively. Mix well and, as soon as it is incorporated, pour it into a greased tray and leave to cool. That should give you a chewy, buttery, lovely toffee.

Panellist pick: ***The best box sets and food to eat while watching***

Sophie Wright recommends *The West Wing*. You've got seven fine seasons to get your teeth into, and to go with them, there's little more fitting than Chinese. In the series, Chinese takeaway features a lot, served in the characteristic American-style fold-out cardboard boxes and eaten with chopsticks. Go for Singapore rice noodles or a General Tso's chicken, classics of Chinese-American cookery.

Dr Annie Gray agrees completely and says we all need a bit of Rob Lowe in a tux. But she also has a soft spot for *Buffy the Vampire Slayer*. Suitable snacks? A bloody stake (!).

Jay Rayner's pick is the French showbiz drama *Call My Agent*. While he says he's not entirely against Gabriel's stress response of squirty cream sprayed straight into his mouth, what really makes the show is its portrait of bourgeois Parisian life. So, it would have to be a cassoulet, or even just a baguette with a round of Camembert, all sent on its way by a big-fisted red from Bordeaux.

Food in space

On the north bank of the River Soar as you head out of Leicester city centre, you'll find the National Space Centre, home to a planetarium, a selection of moon rocks (sadly not made of cheese) and some really big rockets. We're told the most-asked visitor question is how do you go to the loo in space, a theme we can all sympathise with. However, we're more interested in the other end. In the audience at our Space Centre show we welcomed curator **Dan Kendall**, who opened our eyes to the exacting science behind eating in micro-gravity conditions on your way to the moon (and back).

'Before anybody had even been into space, the big concern was whether it was even going to be possible to eat when you were up there.' – Dan Kendall

When Yuri Gagarin became the first human in space on 12 April 1961, he also became the first human to eat in space. He managed two tubes of liver and beef paste and a tube of chocolate to wash it down with. Not exactly gourmet. Dan explained that there were huge concerns over whether you'd be able to swallow in the weightless atmosphere of a space shuttle, so early foods were designed to be squirted straight into an astronaut's mouth. Dehydrated food was used on other early voyages, including tuna salad (which looks a lot like a block of bad pâté when the moisture has been removed).

Crumbs are an issue, too. On *Gemini 3*, John Young and Gus Grissom smuggled in a corned beef sandwich – but two bites in realised there was an issue. Tiny bits of bread floating around in space can get into all sorts of places you don't want them – not so much underfoot, as in your eyes and in delicately tuned machinery. It's not a great idea.

Prof. Barry Smith has worked with the UK Space Agency, and with Heston Blumenthal and his team in the experimental kitchen. Heston's team were invited to devise something less terrible than most space food, but which would still meet all the various regulations. The Fat Duck Team worked directly with Tim Peake, who was the first British astronaut to visit the International Space Station in 2015–16, to tailor a menu specifically to his needs – and likes.

Barry gave the panel a mini experience of eating in space by making us put clothes pegs on our noses and playing loud white noise. The lack of gravity means fluid in the body rises to the head, bunging up the sinuses and disrupting the sense of smell. Meanwhile, the noise, which comes from all the machinery and fans keeping the astronauts alive, can also interfere with our ability to taste. Tim Anderson, Nisha Katona and Andi Oliver all concurred that it was a very weird experience. They ate a version of Tim Peake's bacon sandwich, made with tins left over from the mission and supplied by the UK Space Agency. Tim said you could still taste the bacon because of the umami, while Nisha pointed out you suddenly appreciated the texture (which was designed to be entirely without crumbs).

I fly quite a lot as my family is very far-flung. I always dread the food. Can anyone suggest anything I can do to help myself?

It's fair to say that most of us won't have the pleasure of bacon sarnies in space. But many of us will find ourselves eating in the sky. Barry Smith says it's a notoriously difficult situation in which to serve food. You've got dry, cold cabin air, high altitude, low pressure, all of which mean the flavour molecules act in different ways to your favourite restaurant back on the ground. Plus, you're usually crammed in with others in an emotionally charged space. You can't do much about any of that. However, there is one thing you can change, and that is the noise. White noise of more than 89 decibels affects the brain's ability to process the tastes of sweet and salty, reducing them by about 15%. So, in the air, you're more likely to reach for the salt and sugar to compensate for what, to you, tastes just a little bit bland.

But Barry wants you to try an experiment, if you have some noise-cancelling earphones to hand. Sit at a table, knife and fork in hand, and play airplane background noise (it's amazing what you can find on the internet). Now try eating something (he fed us a cheesecake). Taste OK? Possibly not. Now try your earphones. They work by cancelling out the background noise, not just blocking it, so they will take away a lot of the ambient noise. Now eat again. And ... Andi Oliver tried this on stage and agreed it was remarkable how much difference it made.

If you don't have any fancy headphones, there is another tip in Prof. Barry's book. Umami, the fifth taste, isn't affected in the same way by white noise. So, pick foods high in it – Parmesan or other cheeses, mushrooms, tomatoes, miso, those deeply savoury flavours we tend to gravitate towards. Many people do it naturally, opting for a Bloody Mary or a tomato juice when offered a drink, when they'd normally veer towards gin and tonic or a lime juice.

There's one tiny travelling metal box we haven't touched upon yet: submarines. Nobody has ever asked us anything about submarines, and to be honest it's not exactly a hot topic. But Jocky Petrie's submarine story serves as an excellent example of how culinary wizardry can lead you to unexpected places. He once worked with the crew of HMS *Turbulent*, looking to improve rations for the 120 submariners on board this nuclear submarine. One of the techniques they trialled was sous-vide, where foods are sealed in vacuum packs and cooked to perfection, so that they can just be easily reheated when on board. One of the other advantages is that vac-packed food takes up much less space, and it doesn't need chilling.

The food idea, says Jocky, didn't quite work out. But the captain really embraced the vac-packs. Submarines of that class have to carry a million pounds in cash with them in case war breaks out and they have to go on land and buy extra provisions. It takes up a remarkably large amount of room. So, the vac-packs stayed, but instead of macaroni or mousseline potatoes, they were sealed around a million pounds in money.

Top tip: *Synergistic umami*

We mention umami a lot. It's the fifth taste, sitting alongside salt, sweet, sour and bitter, and it's the kind of savoury flavour you find in Parmesan, soy sauce and mushrooms. But Barry Smith goes one better. He waxes lyrical about synergistic umami: when you have umami from two different families, which then combine to make something truly sublime. So, you might have glutamates: tomatoes, cheese, mushrooms, peas, and these combine with nucleotides: seafood or meat. When you put the two together, you get some of the world's great classics: eggs and bacon, tomato and anchovy, cheese and ham, and scallops and pea purée. Here's to the greatness of synergistic umami.

Science: *The Marmite experiment*

Think the love/hate Marmite marketing ploy is actually true? Think again. Barry Smith has a cunning experiment. He did it on the panel, feeding them all Marmite on a bit of neutral-tasting cracker. We dutifully ate, tasted, swallowed. Then he played us a piece of music, specially commissioned for this, The Great Marmite Experiment. It was instrumental, electronic, with heavy beats. We ate, tasted, swallowed. And then he played us a second piece, quieter, with piano chords. And (you've got it), we ate, tasted, swallowed. By changing the music, he changed the experience: salty, heavy and tangy for the first and fruity, rich and sweet for the second. It's usually the tanginess that people dislike. These pieces were specially commissioned from musician Russ Jones, so it isn't simple to replicate at home. But have a go! Play your breakfast guests some soothing strings and see if they purr. (Other yeast-extract spreads are available, but it may not work with all of them. Let us know if you try it; we'd be interested in the results.)

Salty snacks

The Kitchen Cabinet is well known for its love of salty snacks. If it's crunchy and salty and can be eaten by the handful or the bucketful, we are into it. Crisps are definitely one of our preferred poisons, but let's look beyond the obvious, at other types of salty snacks.

Starting locally, Leicester is the home of Cofresh, the largest provider of Bombay mix in the UK. **Priyesh Patel**, son of the founder, explained that it started when his father took over a fish and chip shop but, being vegetarian, pivoted to make Indian snacks for the local market instead. He started with green peas and peanuts, and ended with a range of mixes – Bombay, Balti, London and Delhi – all based on a mixture of pulses, noodles and nuts with different flavourings added. Making something that would appeal to all races, religions and mainstream consumers was not the easiest of tasks.

I was vegetarian for a couple of years, and then fell off the wagon briefly, during which time I rediscovered my love of pork scratchings. I'm back on the wagon now, though, so can anyone help me to scratch my itch without any animal products?

Meaty flavours are immensely popular to add extra umami to salty snacks. Many of them prove, on careful inspection of the ingredients, to be more vegetarian than you might think, mainly due to the helpful way in which MSG can be used to mimic meaty back notes without being, in fact, meat. So flavouring isn't really an issue when you're looking for a meat-free alternative to something like a pork scratching. It's more about the crunch.

Prof. Peter Barham suggests using a vegan gelling agent – pectin, guar and the like – with fizzy water, to make something that resembles skin. You'd need to dehydrate it, and then deep-fry it. That should give you a good texture, but you will definitely need to go large on the flavouring.

Sophie Wright suggests using seaweed. It's easier to work with – or indeed to buy ready-made – and a deep-fried seaweed has naturally occurring umami. Rice puffs would also work to replicate the crunch. The trouble is, as Tim Hayward points out, once you've had a real scratching, it's very hard to find something convincing. He says some of their appeal is knowing they aren't exactly good for you, so seek out something with the same feeling. How about the scraggly bits of batter from the scrapings of the fryer in the local chip shop? They're usually given away, or at least sold cheaply, and are known as scraps, bits, scrumps, scrags or screeds, depending on where in the country you hail from. Add salt and enjoy.

I've noticed a thing in restaurants for puffy pork scratchings, a bit like a prawn cracker. How can I make them at home?

Whether it's bacon, sausages or crackling, it's fair to say we're huge fans of vitamin P. Nothing beats that porcine goodness, but it's also true that the best bits are not easy to replicate at home. We're often asked about making pork scratchings, and it's a surprisingly complicated topic. They're very much a Black Country speciality, so when we visited the Black Country Living Museum, we made sure to give them much consideration (we ate a lot, in other words). In the audience, we welcomed **Philip Rolls** of Black Country Snacks, a company that has won multiple prizes in the wonderfully named Pork Idol Awards.

Philip explained that there is more than one type of pork scratching. They're a snack with strong working-class associations, from when most rural families (and quite a few urban ones) kept a pig. Come killing day, the saying that you could eat everything but the squeak really was true. So, scratchings were made from the skin, yes, but also from the leaf, or flead, fat. Leaf lard is from the inside of the pig and is the fat that sits around the kidneys and loin. When it's rendered down to make lard, the various bits that don't render out into soft, white lard, crisp up (ish) and become leaf scratchings. They are softer and more obviously fat than the hard scratchings we're used to, and very, very regional. They sell phenomenally in the very small area around the factory and almost not at all beyond it.

More classic scratchings are made from skin, plus the layer of fat underneath. Tim Hayward has experimented with a lot of methods, wielding hairdryers and brine buckets in the name of good taste. He says the secret is to get them really dry. There are various methods – leaving them uncovered in the fridge works well, boiling them briefly in beer first, even better (the aforementioned hairdryer is also good, but time-consuming). Some people remove the fat from the skin, boil or steam it, then dry and fry. Tim's method is simpler: just cubes of skin with the fat still attached, done slowly in the oven first, to dry the skin and render the fat, before deep-frying for maximum crispiness. Then add your salt and any other flavourings you need.

And then there are the puffy ones – chicharrones. Tim Anderson says they are popular in South America as well as most of Asia. To make those, you need to scrape off as much of the fat as possible, leaving only rind. They are normally then deep-fried, sometimes several times, to get the translucent puffy texture. Tim says they are definitely crunchy, but can lack flavour as the fat has been removed. Philip Rolls agrees – they sell all three types of scratching, and their secret is a thing called roast pork seasoning. We did ask, but sadly all was not to be revealed.

Lost in space? Here's some more, for you to write your thoughts.

Pumpkin and squash

By the end of this month, we really can't ignore the encroach of autumn any more. The leaves are turning glorious colours, the nights are getting nippy, and there's a whole host of brightly coloured gourds in every window that can find an excuse for it. It's squash season, not just pumpkins but, let's face it, they're the one on most of our minds.

Every Hallowe'en I get perplexed by pumpkins. I like carving them, sometimes with my kids, and, let's face it, also alone, but then I feel I should eat the flesh and save waste and it is always underwhelming. Is it me?

Pity poor unaware pumpkin purchasers. If you buy a thing called a carving pumpkin, they really are just for carving. They're grown for size, says Lizzie Mabbott. Yes, you can try cooking with them, but they will take forever, and have no flavour at the end of it. And you can try roasting the pumpkin seeds, but, again, you'll be destined for disappointment.

It's a shame, for there are some incredible pumpkin dishes out there if you get one grown for substance, rather than just style. Lizzie's very fond of the wide range of Asian desserts made with pumpkin. Try cubing it, cooking it with coconut milk, sago and taro and serving it chilled or hot. Or purée it with mango, or jelly it, or even make it into a sweet egg custard, which looks particularly lovely served in steamed baby pumpkins that you can slice and eat.

When we visited Spalding, in Lincolnshire, we met **Jonathan Nicholls**, a pumpkin carving expert who brought us our very own Jay Rayner-kin, featuring Jay's face engraved large and grinning on a brightly coloured fruit. He uses the seeds from his pumpkins, roasting them with honey and cinnamon.

Jordan Bourke says it's a great use for pumpkin seeds and adds that his top tip for the faff of removing the flesh from the seeds is the classic 1980s salad spinner. Get really aggressive with it, and it'll help a lot.

Annie Gray says the history of pumpkin carving is pretty recent. There are lots of different strands that go into creating it, and it's hard to untangle them all. If you look for the origins, you'll read all sorts of stories linking pumpkin lanterns with a man called Jack, who apparently offended heaven and hell and roamed the earth with a coal stuck in a pumpkin. But the word 'jack-o'-lantern' in terms of a pumpkin, or any other form of vegetable, comes from the nineteenth century, and originally meant 'a man with a lantern', just as a 'jack-of-all-trades' was 'a man who did lots of things': 'jack' just means 'man', but the term came to be applied to marsh gas or will-o'-the-wisp. The idea and name are kind of catchy, and what they caught onto was another strand, which is a load of folk rituals around evil spirits and carving things. In Somerset, it was spunkies or punkies, made from turnips carved like gargoyles – they don't necessarily seem to have been hollowed out. And the Irish tradition, which was similar, went over to the States, met the – much, much easier to carve – native pumpkins, and came back again to rejoin all the rest. Annie says if you're keen to avoid waste when carving something for Hallowe'en, try a turnip (though she doesn't actually recommend it, unless you have a lot of patience).

Squash: love the idea, don't know what to do with them beyond mashing. Can the panel help, please?

There are lots of squash bred for good eating. Jordan Bourke has a Hallowe'en hotpot for which he uses Delicia (you could also use other winter squash, such as Crown Prince, Turban or the huge, craggy French Musquée de Provence). Just scoop out the seeds and add some bread, cream, stock, herbs, seasonings and cheese. Put the whole thing in the oven and cook until perfectly tender. It's gorgeous to look at, and when you eat it, you just scoop out the filling with all the soft flesh as well. If you want an extra Hallowe'en thrill, leave it in the oven just a little bit longer and it'll collapse in a scary Hallowe'en heap of molten cheese.

Shelina Permalloo does a Sri Lankan pumpkin curry: chopped, skin-on pumpkin, a load of coconut milk, desiccated coconut (this will bloom and thicken, really enriching the curry), cardamom, chilli, turmeric, black cardamom if you have it, cinnamon sticks, plenty of salt and curry leaves. Simmer this for 45 minutes, and finish with some mustard oil. The skin on the pumpkin will soften up, giving it a textural contrast. Pumpkin skin is used a lot in Sri Lanka – think chutneys, pickles etc.

Peel is great, agrees Niki Segnit. She uses it to pep up butternut squash soup, which can be bland. Try using the peel in the way you'd use bones to make stock. Just cook it with a little bit of tomato purée and some leeks, a touch of fennel and black peppercorn and a dash of white wine. For added flavour, add a pinch of cayenne pepper – and roast your squash first to get some nice Maillard reaction going. All those caramelised bits really help.

Jeremy Pang reckons roasting is the way to go. He was inspired by Nisha Katona roasting whole swedes as a meat stand-in. His version is a roast butternut squash char siu.

Butternut char siu

Just quarter the squash and score it diagonally on the flesh side. Then make a sauce. You want to riff on the idea of a ratio, using 2:1 thick to thin. Thick ingredients might be hoi sin, ketchup or sugar, while thin ingredients are dark soy and rice vinegar. Pour this all over, and then roast the squash for 45 minutes before finishing by charring it under the grill (you can also barbecue it if we get a sudden Indian summer).

Top tip: ***Why you should never put your eggs in the fridge***

Peter Barham says you may think it prolongs their life, but it destroys their flavour and texture. By putting your eggs in the fridge, you're changing the temperature of the egg a lot, up and down whenever you open the door. Eggs are permeable to air, water, CO_2 – and in the fridge you destabilise them, encouraging them to suck in the aromas of whatever is around them, from kippers to mouldy vegetables. Keep them in a room without such major temperature fluctuations and they'll be much happier, take in less of their environment, and they'll be just fine to eat for a very long time.

Top tip: ***Whether to prick our sausages***

Tim Hayward says it sort of doesn't matter. If you prick, they won't burst, but you'll let the fat out. Then again, if you're frying them, you'll be putting the fat back in from the frying anyway. Sophie Wright agrees that it doesn't matter if they burst and you really shouldn't worry. But if you prefer them unburst, the secret is to precook them. Poach them (she likes to do it in beer) and then grill (or fry) them. They will stay plump and moist, they won't burst all over the pan, and you'll still get the crispy brown on the outside, while being perfectly cooked in the middle.

Finally, we asked our audience in Blackpool about their edible Hallowe'en traditions.

More than a few of you admitted to putting the lights off and hiding under a blanket with your own choice of spooky snacks. But, really, kudos to the family who make frozen severed jelly hands – the trick? Make them in a rubber glove.

November

Wrap up warm and sally forth for these hot dates:

Día de los Muertos (celebrating ancestors with their favourite foods. Also, excellent skull-themed edibles of many and varied kinds)

Bonfire Night (toffee apples and parkin and burning effigies on bonfires)

St Martin's Day/Martinmas (reputedly a good time to slaughter cattle before winter feed shortages)

Clovelly Herring Festival (celebrating the 'silver darlings')

Stir-up Sunday (a tongue-in-cheek Victorian invention, made much of in more recent years)

BBC Good Food Show, autumn edition

The Cake & Bake Show, London (and elsewhere)

The moon this month is made of **Baron Bigod**

Brie is big in the UK, and at its best in the autumn. Brie de Meaux is the one with the PDO, made in glorious 3kg wheels with unpasteurised cows' milk. But Bungay-made Baron Bigod gives any Brie a run for its money, and far outpaces the plastic stuff found in so many disappointing sandwiches. Raw or baked, it is squidgy and flavoursome, great with dried fruit or just squashed onto bread. The rind is fully edible too.

This month *The Kitchen Cabinet* is in **Brixton**, known for its African-Caribbean community, bustling market full of global goods and rich retail heritage.

Key flavours include **chard**, **cabbage**, **sloes** and **parsnips**, plus **herring** and **wild game**.

And we are also thinking about:

- Yorkshire puddings
- How to make toffee apples
- The difference between ghee and clarified butter
- To salt or not to salt when boiling vegetables

- And whether lasagne gets better when you leave it overnight

---

Welcome to Brixton in South London. Home of the first purpose-built department store in the UK, and one of the first streets to be lit with electricity – if you aren't humming 'Electric Avenue' by now, you should be. Also home to a thriving African-Caribbean community since the first of the *Windrush* generation arrived in the 1940s, it's a food paradise for anyone after the flavours of the West Indies and many of our panel can wax lyrical for hours on the subject of Brixton Market, which includes both open-air stalls and the 1920s and 1930s Grade II-listed covered arcades in the surrounding streets. More recently, the global food scene has exploded in Brixton, and the arcades – rebranded Brixton Village – now hold a host of small restaurants offering everything from Portuguese to Japanese cuisine.

Caribbean flavours

In 1948, the *Empire Windrush* docked at Tilbury in Essex, carrying 802 Commonwealth citizens from the Caribbean. They were the first of around half a million Commonwealth workers to settle in the UK in the wake of the British Nationality Act, which aimed to encourage immigration to help rebuild the nation after the Second World War. Those who came in were promised full and equal rights of citizenship and encouraged to be patriotic and join nationalised employers, such as the fledgling NHS, British Rail and the Post Office. With an acute housing shortage in London following the Blitz, many of the new arrivals were initially housed in an underground shelter in Clapham South, finding work in the areas nearby, and eventually making Brixton a small hub of Caribbean culture. The *Empire Windrush* didn't just bring people though – the rich culinary heritage of the Caribbean came too. Seventy years later, some of the dishes they brought – jerk chicken, rice and peas, ackee and saltfish – have become well known far beyond the communities they started in.

I live in a very small flat: no barbecue, dodgy oven. How can I make a really good jerk chicken?

We thought we'd talk jerk upfront, as it is such an icon of the Caribbean in the UK. It's the national dish of Jamaica, and is based on a specific (and sometimes hotly debated) spice blend, which can be used as a seasoning or as the basis for a marinade, not just for chicken, but for pork, for prawns, for anything you fancy. The exact spices vary, but allspice is crucial, plus chilli. After that, it's up to you. Dried herbs, cumin, ginger, pepper, sugar, they all find their way in. The meat was traditionally cooked over an open fire, often using wood from the allspice tree, and giving it a distinctive smoked flavour as well as a blackened skin.

In the audience in Brixton we welcomed **Brian Danclair**, of Brixton restaurant Fish, Wings & Tings. He says the key to a good jerk anything is a long marinade. He adds fresh chilli, spring onion and onion to his basic rub (among other things) and advises leaving it for at least a day, preferably two. He suggests grilling it high – you want a really dark skin.

Tim Hayward agrees that heat is crucial. Try putting a paving slab or a bakestone in the bottom of your oven to really retain and even out the heat. Jerk also tends to have a smoky flavour, hard to obtain in a domestic environment. He has a glass smoking bottle he persuaded one of the specialist suppliers to the University of Cambridge labs to make him. The 'smoking bottle' has a small 'cup' at the top with a long tube going into liquid in the bottle below. There is a tube, coming out of the side of the bottle above liquid level, where you can suck to reduce the air pressure. This sucks the smoke down, to bubble up through the liquid. It is, in every respect, a bong. Smokers use such apparatus to cool the smoke before inhaling. He uses it with a vacuum pump instead, to infuse any liquid with smoke. He says you could use a hookah, hubble-bubble pipe or commercially made bong. You can also buy semi-professional smoke generators. Or you could just use a commercially smoked oil in your marinade.

Smoke isn't that vital, says Andi Oliver. Don't get obsessed with it if you can't make it happen. The real point is the flavour. She says definitely make your own seasoning – or if you do buy a base from a shop, zack it up when you make it into a marinade. Citrus is particularly helpful. A good slug of orange juice, lime and lemon really helps to stop it getting muddy. She also adds fresh ginger, again for the zing. And for even more added flavour, serve it with a fiery syrup – just sugar syrup, fresh ginger, red chilli flakes and orange juice, plus a bit of cinnamon and star anise.

If you are doing jerk by marinating, Dr Zoe Laughlin says one of the main aims is to tenderise the meat. With marinades of any kind, you can go one of two ways. Either pick something acid to add to your seasoning mix, like the citrus Andi uses, or something that will soften the meat enzymatically. That means ginger, papaya, pineapple, kiwi. Just be careful how much you consume – she has a friend who ended up dissolving the inside of her mouth with her over-enthusiastic kiwi consumption.

I love jerk chicken, but I want to go further. Can the panel suggest some classic Caribbean dishes I can make to wow my mates?

Brian Danclair was very happy to hear this. He explained that the Caribbean is a catch-all term for very different places. There are thousands of islands, and 26 countries. He hails from Trinidad, but you've also got Barbados, Jamaica, Antigua, St Kitts and Guyana.

All have quite distinct cuisines – thus ackee is really Jamaican. In Antigua, the main accompaniment to saltfish is chop-up, an aubergine-rich vegetable stew. There's also fungee, based on cornmeal and not unlike a thick, cornmeal porridge, eaten with butter. Then there's Antiguan pepperpot, a meat stew with vegetables such as spinach, aubergine and greens, plus dried pigeon peas. Guyana has its own version, also called pepperpot, but very different. There, it's usually made of mutton, goat or pork, plus a deep, chilli-fired sweetish sauce, the crucial ingredient for which is cassareep. Cassareep is made of bitter cassava, an ingredient that, unprocessed, can be very toxic. Buy cassareep, don't make your own.

One of the key features of Caribbean cuisine is the way in which it mixes Old World influences with the ingredients native to the area, and the culinary heritage of the African diaspora. Andi Oliver says have a crack at vina dosh, a Caribbean cousin of vindaloo, both derived from the fifteenth-century Portuguese dish vinha d'alhos (meat with wine vinegar and garlic).

Vina dosh

Take your meat – a pork cheek is ideal – and marinate it in thyme, garlic, nutmeg and allspice – lovely things like that. Add chopped onion, chopped gooseberries and vinegar, and leave it for a few days in the fridge, turning it every so often. Then slow roast it. You'll find all the acid in the vinegar and the gooseberries helps break down the meat and makes it really tender. When it's cooked, just reduce down the liquid you've got left and it'll make a beautiful sauce.

If you want a good accompaniment for your meat stews, you can't really go wrong with rice and peas. If you've got the image of bright white rice with little green peas in it, think again. Rice and peas is rice and dried pulses, either black-eyed peas, red beans or pigeon peas. It's easy too, especially if you have pre-cooked beans. Just cook the rice in coconut milk, add a bit of thyme, tiny bit of onion, season with salt and then add your beans. If you're using dried beans, cook them first, along with the thyme and onion, until they are about three-quarters done, then add the coconut milk and rice and finish the cooking. Salt to taste at the end. Andi Oliver says it's one of the recipes she will pass onto her kids.

On the subject of beans, Tim Anderson says it's fine to use tinned beans. When you buy dried pulses, you risk having them from different batches, and it's hard to get them all cooked to perfection, even with a pressure cooker. Angela Hartnett disagrees. She says the tinned type tend to be slimy, and she'd rather spend the time soaking them and cooking from scratch. Just don't season until the end as the salt will make them toughen up.

Top tip: *How to make a toffee apple*

Sophie Wright tells us how to make a toffee apple that isn't just mushy apple and over-soft toffee. Use a small, firm apple, such as a Pippin, something you can get your jaw round, but which has a good, crisp texture. A floury apple will start to cook when you pour on the toffee and that's what makes it go mushy. Then you want to make a caramel of 225g sugar and 110ml water. Dissolve the sugar in the water on a medium heat and then add 25g of butter, 2 tablespoons golden syrup and ½ teaspoon cider vinegar, which will help it set and stop it crystallising. Take the mixture almost to hard crack – 140°C – which should take around 10 minutes. Pour this over your apple and leave to set. Remember to put them on baking parchment to set, or they will stick like crazy.

If, however, like Tim Anderson, you feel a toffee apple is an inefficient toffee and apple delivery device, you can serve softer toffee as a dip on the side. Or go for Jeremy Pang's toffee apple sausage, which is a sausage (a pork and apple one if you want to be pedantic, though when he made it for us it was a frankfurter) in a spun sugar spring. Do try this at home.

Rice

If you're lamenting your lack of dried pulses to make rice and peas, don't worry. Rice is a subject that comes up a lot on the programme. Jeremy Pang admits to being a *fàntǒng*, or 'rice bucket', someone who could happily eat rice for every meal for ever. But we are all partial to a good rice pudding, a risotto or just a bowl of fluffy white loveliness on the side.

I've recently moved house and finally have space to expand my store cupboard. But I'm not sure how many rice types I actually need. Before I rush out and fill my shelves, what do the panel advise?

Prof. Barry Smith says the key difference between rice types isn't just the size of the grain – short, medium and long – but the starches. In long-grain rice you have amylose, which is one of the polysaccharides. Straight amylose chains break down when you cook them at a high temperature and they absorb water. They become less densely packed and you easily get separate grains of rice, which are springy and pretty much your archetypal plain boiled rice. But they harden when they cool. When you look at short-grain rice, its starch is mostly amylopectin, which is a very different polysaccharide, and tends to clump together after heating. As you break down these curly chains of granule molecules, they clump and get sticky – which is why we get sticky rice from short-grain rice. It stays soft as it cools, which is why it is used in sushi. It is glutenous in texture but has no actual gluten. It is just gloopy and sticky. Medium-grain rice has half the amount of amylose as long-grain rice.

For Korean cuisine, you need a medium-grain rice, explains Jordan Bourke. It's chewy, retaining a lot of moisture. Rice is synonymous with eating, so much so that when you greet someone in Korea, you use the phrase '*Bap meo-geo-seo-yo?*', which literally translates as 'Have you eaten rice/a meal?' A plain 'How are you?' would be missing the point – if you haven't eaten, you clearly aren't well. The Koreans also eat the short-grain sticky (glutinous) rice, known as sweet rice, though it can, of course, be used in savoury dishes too.

Short-grain rice is the type used in the UK for rice puddings, precisely because of its clumping properties. Sophie Wright says look for proper pudding rice – it's got one of the shortest grains going. Then cook it low and slow: 3 hours in a buttered dish in an oven will do it, and all you need add to it is milk, a tiny bit of sugar and maybe a bit of cinnamon. A tablespoon of rice to a pint of milk is pretty standard.

If you do want to jazz up a rice pudding, Andi Oliver cooks hers with two parts coconut milk to one part cream and starts it off on the hob to get it to the boil – it cuts down the oven time considerably. She then sugars the top and treats it like a crème brûlée. For extra jazz, she adds a mango rum syrup, but it depends on just how jazzy you feel a rice pudding should be.

Risotto. How do I make it without having to buy a new pan each time I cook it?

Low and slow applies to more than just pudding. Risotto is a running theme for our TKC audiences. Dr Annie Gray does hers in a pressure cooker and swears by it, but the rest of the panel were unconvinced.

Sophie Wright's a traditionalist. She spent time in Italy, learning from the village *nonna*. A big surface area is crucial: don't use a saucepan. Instead, look for a skillet or deep frying pan. You do need to stir it, she says, no way round it, in a figure of eight, and it is going to take 17–22 minutes. Tim Anderson disagrees. He says it is all about the moisture. So, sauté your onions and garlic, using lots of butter or olive oil. Add your rice to get it toasted and covered with fat, and control the heat. Don't blast it or it will stick. Then you can add your stock, gradually, keeping it wet, wet, wet. As to the stirring, you do need to stir, but not constantly. Keep it bubbling and move it a bit until it is pretty much cooked. Only then do you reduce it down and chuck in loads of cheese.

Sue Lawrence's tip is on the type of rice. Most people use arborio, but carnaroli is much better, for it doesn't get stodgy if you accidentally overcook it.

There's a school of thought that says risotto should take hours, but she agrees with Sophie, 20 minutes is really optimum – more than that and your rice will be ruined. At the end, really beat in the finishing ingredients: cold butter, Parmesan (unless it is a seafood risotto), breaking up all the starches and getting that lovely dairy lusciousness. And don't just dump it on a plate, either. Serve it, as the Italians say, *all'onda*, 'in a wave'.

Science: *Yorkshire puddings*

On one of our Leeds shows, Rob Owen-Brown and Zoe Laughlin teamed up to try the Yorkshire Pudding Eggsperiment. Rob made three Yorkshire puds: one with one egg, one with two, and one with three. Zoe put them on trivets and poured gravy on top. Which would win? Which would absorb more gravy? Zoe says Yorkshire puddings are really a vehicle for gravy delivery and management. They need heft, weight and ... the one egg one collapsed before she'd finished explaining. The second started dripping. The three-egger proved her point: always over-egg the (Yorkshire) pudding.

But Zoe didn't stop there. She had a six-egger on stage, something you could almost live in. Not only that, it was made in the shape of a gravy boat. It's her ultimate dream: a gravy-boat Yorkie. Imagine ... you pour it, you enjoy the gravy (and then some more gravy), and then, as the anticipation peaks, and the meal is almost over, you have a Yorkshire pudding gravy chaser to divide up at the end.

Top tip: ***Leaving lasagne overnight***

Zoe Laughlin says it's true that lasagne tastes better the next day, and there's science to back it up. As the proteins break down in the fridge overnight, they release amino acids, which taste extra delicious. Even if yours is a vegetarian lasagne, you'll still get extra sugars released from the starch the second time you cook it, increasing that all important browning. It will genuinely taste better the second time around.

Top tip: ***Why you don't need to salt vegetables when cooking***

Prof. Peter Barham says he's heard all sorts of arguments: it adds flavour, it raises the boiling point, it fixes the colour. But these are all wrong. It does nothing apart from waste salt and energy. Vegetables aren't boiled for long enough to absorb any flavour, and the salt is just rinsed away with the water (unless you use Victorian boiling times, which, well, just don't). The only exception is potatoes, which are starchy and do take on some added flavour.

Head buzzing? Here's a handy space to scribble down your ideas.

Gingerbread

We've talked about putting ginger in your jerk, but that's not the only reason it's on our minds. Ginger's one of the big hitters in sweet baking at this time of year. Whether you're particular to parkin, go crazy for cake or just like biting the heads off gingerbread people, autumn's when gingerbreads really come into their own.

Sticky licky gingerbread or crunchy crispy biscuits: what's the panel's preference?

Nearly every region has a ginger speciality, says Annie Gray. Historically, ginger was one of the cheaper spices, and so was widely used. But early gingerbreads contained other spices too. Medieval recipes can be pretty basic – just breadcrumbs, honey and a blend of spices, which included cinnamon and pepper. They were sometimes coloured red or yellow. By the seventeenth century, baked, flour or oat-based versions were gaining in popularity, with oaty gingerbreads more dominant in the North, and wheat favoured in the South. There were as many recipes as there were towns, and various excellent excuses were dreamt up to make and eat them. In Grasmere, gingerbread was part of the rush-bearing ceremonies in the local church, and was probably the soft, sticky style we think of as cake today. The modern shortbread-like Grasmere gingerbread took off in the 1850s. Meanwhile, in Yorkshire a hefty treacle-based version called pepper cake was the thing to eat on Christmas Eve well into the twentieth century. Further south, in Grantham, a crisp, hollow biscuit became part of the town's heritage, selling to the hordes of travellers who changed coaches on their way up the Great North Road (now, less poetically, the A1).

Annie brought us an eighteenth-century ginger biscuit to try, which Tim Hayward described as looking and feeling like a cross between a bullet and sheep poo. It was, indeed, rather rocklike. But, as Annie explained, many of the recipes from that era were intended for long keeping and softened over time. Hers included coriander seed, caraway, cloves and finely minced peel. But she says her favourite is a nineteenth-century ginger cake, which uses an entire tin of treacle, plus butter, flour, eggs, milk and ginger. It keeps indefinitely and makes a fabulous crumble topping.

Sophie Wright agrees. She's been experimenting with using tinned pumpkin purée in her ginger cakes, where it adds moisture and flavour, just like in a carrot cake. If you prefer to make it yourself, you can roast the purée at home. When you add it to your cake, use a bit of buttermilk as well, which will really enrich it. Cakes like this are easily made gluten-free by using brown rice flour or buckwheat flour. This all sounds very familiar to Tim Anderson, who has a version from *The Anderson Family Cookbook*, the ring-bound repository of family recipes that is a regular and beloved feature on the show. He says the pumpkin really adds moisture – you can also use squash.

Tim has a soft spot for the harder types of gingerbread as well. They are more versatile, especially blitzed up as a basis for other things, and they go really well with cheese. And, of course, you can cut them into shapes. Zoe Laughlin had a lot of fun making a suitably TKC-themed gingerbread biscuit, settling on a Jay-shaped stencil to be used with a standard gingerbread man cutter. With icing sifted through it, Jay's bearded face appeared, giving us the impassive face he uses to make us shut up when we talk too much. A Jaygerbread, if you will. Spicy.

Which is better to use in my baking: stem ginger, ground ginger, crystallised ginger or a combination of the three?

Shelina Permalloo spreads the ginger love. She says use all three, especially in a ginger cake. One of her *Masterchef* recipes was a knockout ginger cake, which used dried ginger, stem ginger and fresh ginger in the cake itself, plus ground ginger run through the salted caramel syrup she poured on top.

Different types have different properties, says Sophie Wright. Fresh will give you a tang, and a sharp, spicy hit. Ground is universally called for in recipes and it is an easy go-to. But if you've only got space for one, she favours stem ginger. You can use the syrup as well as the ginger itself, and it never goes off due to the high sugar content. When we went to Blenheim Palace, we met the then Head Butler, **Stephen Duckett**, who fed us his version of an after-dinner palate cleanser. It was just laser-thin slices of stem ginger, coated in sugar, and dried out very slowly on an old hot plate. Tim Hayward took the rest home with him.

Tim Anderson has a good use for the syrup from your stem ginger: how about a gingerbread Manhattan? It's basically a classic Manhattan, so bourbon or rye, dry vermouth, a twist of orange peel, and then a sugar syrup, which is normally made from stock syrup infused with ginger, star anise and some cloves. But you can use the stem ginger syrup as your base and add other spices as you fancy. Be careful, though. Don't go down the more spice is more seasonal route or you'll fall into the trap of so many coffee chains, with their pumpkin-latte-winter-spice-mocha-chococinos. Tim Hayward says it can be like licking a festive air freshener, and nobody wants that.

Crystallised ginger has its place, argues Andi Oliver, though it tends to knock around, especially after Christmas. She says you should riff around whatever you've got. Steamed or baked puddings are great with a ginger back note: try a standard sponge pudding mix, but line the bowl or tray with a syrup made from treacle, brown sugar, vanilla and rum-soaked sultanas. Try adding a bit of cocoa powder into the batter along with chopped crystallised ginger. Cook it all up and then make a sticky toffee sauce with added rum and cocoa. Chocolate, ginger, rum – a classic combination. She also recommends bulla, which is a Jamaican gingerbread, recipes for which involve every sort of ginger, including fresh.

What's the difference? *Ghee vs clarified butter*

Asma Khan says ghee is not just clarified butter, so stop spreading it on your toast. Clarified butter is just unsalted butter that has been briefly boiled until the milk solids fall to the bottom. It's quick and easy. When you make ghee, you first churn your butter, then drain off the buttermilk, and then leave it overnight, meaning it ferments just slightly. It is then boiled down in a huge pot for a long time until the milk solids caramelise fully, before being strained out. This gives it far more flavour than clarified butter, and it also means that it doesn't need refrigeration, which is very important in a country like India. Ghee uses a lot of milk and it's a time-consuming process, which makes it very expensive. It's used in purification rituals, including a child's first meal, or to rub on the feet of idols in temples. It is not a thing to be used in everyday dishes.

Winter warmers

It's fair to say that the good team TKC has explored most of the regions of the UK in search of a good dinner. We've furkled out forgotten foods and tried hard to shine a light on local specialities. Gingerbread comes up a lot, as do pies. But another of the things nearly every place in the UK has a version of is a stew.

A stew was a 'stove' in medieval English and it became a word for brothel long before it was used to describe a long-cooked casserole. Brothels were associated with public bathhouses, heated, of course, with stoves, so you can see where the links all came from. Just a warning next time you say you fancy a stew for supper.

Annie Gray says the regionality of stews can be over-exaggerated. Regional cuisine is usually based on whatever is in the region, and in a relatively small country such as the UK, there are a lot of similarities between many of the dishes later writers extolled as being distinct to each place. You'll usually find such stews contain a cheap cut of meat (led by the dominant reason for keeping livestock, i.e. wool or dairy); some vegetables, mainly of the allium persuasion (cheap, easy to grow); and something starchy to bulk it all out.

At the point where these things were a staple – and bear in mind they were never a staple for the very poor, who struggled to afford meat at all – there were loads of different versions of each stew, between households, between villages, between towns.

But then we get to the mid-twentieth century, regional cuisine is seen to be dying out, and there's a conscious movement to revalue British cuisine. People start seeking out these regional recipes and write down the last remaining ones. But not only do **well-meaning metropolitan writers have a tendency to believe every random thing the bloke who props up the table in the local pub tells them**, but the very act of writing things down influences the traditions they are trying to save. And so sometimes the version written down becomes set in stone and then we all get obsessed with doing it in the right way.

One of the best-known regional stews is lobscouse, a Liverpudlian concoction of beef or lamb, potatoes and onion. It's related to other, similarly named, dishes – labskaus in Germany, lapskaus in Norway, lapskojs in Sweden. They seem to come from a shared pan-European heritage, probably based on maritime provisions, which spread via seamen as they travelled the trade routes of the time. The term 'scouse' for Liverpudlians came later.

From his position astride the Lancashire–Yorkshire border, Rob Owen-Brown agrees that regional stews are all based on the same idea: take meat, not very good, and cook it very slowly with some stuff to give it flavour, until it falls apart. Thus, Monmouth stew is mutton shoulder, browned off with onion, carrot, celery and lots of leeks, while Staffordshire lobby stew is beef, onions, potatoes and other root vegetables, plus optional pearl barley.

Yet another classic stew is Irish stew. Jordan Bourke says there's a joy to be found in revisiting recipes from your parents' and grandparents' time, but that we shouldn't become too wedded to them.

Irish stew

Jordan's Irish stew uses sliced onion, a few sprigs of thyme and lamb – shoulder or neck is ideal. If you've got the bones, even better. Put all of this in a pan, cover it with water and simmer for 1½ to 2 hours until the meat is tender. Then add peeled and halved potatoes and cook for another 30 minutes. Serve with parsley scattered on top. But Jordan says that while that's the basic recipe, based on what people had at the time, these days we can be a bit more decadent. Maybe add a carrot or, let's face it, anything you like.

Such stews are meant to be pimped, agrees Rachel McCormack. She advises using a local beer instead of water or stock. Or you could add a bit of spice for a back note – Tim Hayward suggests star anise. Meanwhile, one of our audience members in Stoke-on-Trent admitted her go-to was a bit of brown sauce.

I love a good winter warmer, but I'm cutting down on meat, especially red meat. What's a good vegetarian alternative?

Nisha Katona says lentils are the backbone of Indian cuisine, and that a dhal is a brilliant winter warmer.

You've got two types of lentils, the red and yellow ones, which are unhusked, simple to cook, and easy to digest. Try boiling them up with some tomatoes and turmeric until they soften, and then frying some cumin seeds and a little bit of chilli in a separate pan. Finally, combine the two, adding a little lemon juice and salt.

For the heavier lentils – the green, black, brown and puy, there's a different culinary philosophy. They need to cook for up to 3 hours, so start by cooking them down with onion, ginger and garlic, plus cumin seeds. Simmer, simmer, simmer, and then, at the end, you can add in sharper ingredients – rhubarb, extra ginger, even things like preserved lemons.

Rachel McCormack suggests making the most of cauliflower. We all know about cauliflower cheese, but it is also great in a stew. So, try onions, garlic and cauliflower, sweet potato and chestnuts, and then flavour them with herbs (but not the Mallorcan herbal liquor she tried once, don't do that). The thing about stews is the slow-cooking means flavours really combine and they are very forgiving.

And finally, we asked our audience in Newtownards for their family food arguments.

We often find ourselves settling such disputes, but we couldn't really help on this one: peas in a cottage pie. Love them? (The green! The sweet! The pop! The convenience!) Hate them? (The weirdness of finding one! The way they go green! The tiny pea-y bubbles that go pop!) The family was torn. We suggested serving them on the side in the hope of reaching a fragile pea...ce.

MARMALADE

December

The last few dates for this year's food diary:

English Breakfast Day (just add bacon)

Feast of St Nicholas (the eve is focused on shoes, but the day can involve gingerbread)

Hanukkah (latkes and sufganiyot, because nothing says godly like a jam doughnut)

Tom Bawcock's Eve, Mousehole (an excuse to scoff stargazy pie)

Christmas Day (ergo dinner)

St Stephen's Day (leftovers, but also goose pie in the North Riding)

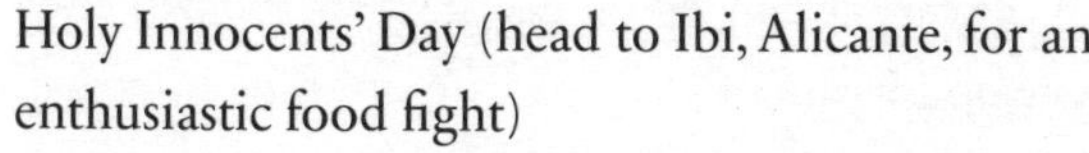

Holy Innocents' Day (head to Ibi, Alicante, for an enthusiastic food fight)

New Year's Eve (goodbye 2022, and here's to a new food year)

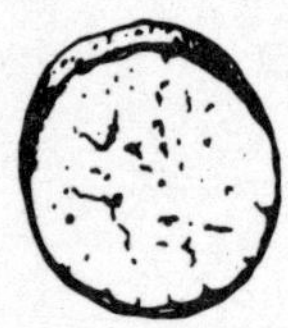   

The moon this month is made of **Stichelton**

A raw milk blue cheese named for the Anglo-Saxon spelling of 'Stilton'. Wheels of Stilton have long been prized, becoming popular first among travellers on the Great North Road who stopped off at the inn where it was sold. But modern Stilton, whose sales peak at Christmas, is made according to the regulations of its PDO, which state that it must use pasteurised milk. Stichelton takes the type back to before widespread use of pasteurisation in the mid-twentieth century and aims to replicate the style of Stilton that George Orwell called 'The best cheese of its type in the world.'

And, in case it's been bugging you for an entire year (OK, book) now, just why do we say the moon is made of cheese? It is rooted in various medieval stories in which someone (or thing) mistakes the reflection of the full moon for a cheese, leading usually to embarrassment, satisfaction or being eaten. By the sixteenth century, it had become a proverb. English poet John Heywood wrote of people trying to dupe him that they were making him think 'that the moone is made of greene cheese.' 'Green' in this case simply meant 'young', not actually green. From then on it was used in the context of someone being fooled – or being foolish. But it's a striking image, and it lived on in popular folklore, eventually becoming a cute thing to tell children rather than a cutting way to impugn someone's intelligence.

This month *The Kitchen Cabinet* is in **Dundee**, known as the home of the *Beano*, the latest outpost of the V&A and as the marmalade capital of the UK.

Key flavours this month include **chestnuts**, **poultry**, **sprouts** and **salsify**.

And we are also thinking about:

- The ideal way to carve a turkey
- Glorious gravy
- How to cook roast potatoes
- Whether a garlic press is naughty or nice
- And how to deshell a hard-boiled egg

Welcome to Dundee: once called the city of 'jute, jam and journalism', it boomed off the back of all three from the mid-nineteenth century. Today the jute is gone, and the jam much reduced. However, DC Thomson, publisher of the *Dandy* (once home to Desperate Dan), the *Beano* and many other titles, is still based in the city, along with other, less onomatopoeic attractions. We ambled the waterfront, admired the modern architecture of the V&A, and then disappeared off in search of Arbroath smokies, and to hunt down some old-style Dundee marmalade.

Glorious gravy

Sometimes on *The Kitchen Cabinet*, food becomes poetry. This is the ballad of Tim Hayward's gravy.

'I think gravy needs a spirit. You need to be thinking about the gravy, right the way through the meat. So, you need to collect your pan juices to begin with. And then I would ordinarily start in a separate pan with a small amount of onion chopped up very, very finely, which I would probably begin to clarify in butter and then add something like port, sherry or Madeira to that, and burn that off, reducing it right the way down to a really sludgy paste. If you want to thicken with flour – some people do, I usually don't – you add a little bit of flour to that and cook that through. Then you add your meat juices and drippings into your pot. That's your basis. And that's where we go completely off-piste because a really, really good gravy has got all of the spirit of the meat in it, all that ...'

'Love?' offers Jay, but no ... 'Ingredients. You need to find balance for a really stonking gravy. Maybe mushroom ketchup or the vinegar from pickled walnuts. Some balsamic vinegar or a touch of honey might go in there to make it sweet, but keep tasting, adding, tasting, adding a bit of pepper, a bit of salt, and you will build and build, and you will make a fine thing.'

Fruit cake

December is a time for hefty flavours and rib-sticking repasts. With Christmas on the horizon, thoughts turn to rich fruit cake – some love it, some hate it – so let's start by talking about Dundee cake, the zesty confection to which the city has given its name.

Time to bust another myth. Dundee cake is first recorded in the 1830s, and has nothing to do with Mary, Queen of Scots and her supposed dislike of candied cherries. We spoke to **Martin Goodfellow**, of Dundee bakery Goodfellow and Steven, who explained that really its roots lie in the marmalade industry, as one of its principal ingredients is candied peel. Dundee-made recipes also contain sultanas, but no other dried fruit. They were almost certainly invented and commercialised by Keiller's, Dundee's major marmalade producer at the time, and until the 1980s a kind of gentleman's agreement seemed to have existed, which meant no other Dundee-based company produced them. However, they were widely copied elsewhere, and other manufacturers put all sorts of things in them, until the only thing that showed they were a Dundee cake was the characteristic pattern of almonds on the top.

Whatever you do, don't put cherries in a Dundee cake. It should be a buttery, orangey sultana cake. Anything else is just plain wrong.

True Dundee cake is a world away from the rich, hefty confection known now as Christmas cake. But it's the latter that gets all the press at this time of year. It's divisive. Dr Annie Gray says it is because we are doing it wrong. Nobody really knows when to eat Christmas cake – it's too much after a large lunch, and it can hang about. She wants us to bring back the Twelfth cake. It's also a rich fruit cake but is associated with Twelfth Night. From the medieval era until the second half of the nineteenth century, Twelfth Night was a really big thing, a chance to send off the festive period with a bang. Twelfth cake was part of this, and by the seventeenth century it was customary to hide tokens in the cake – a bean for the king, a pea for the queen. Later this developed into a set of character cards with riddles in. Twelfth cake rituals feed into both modern Christmas cake and crackers. But the whole thing dwindled and died in the late Victorian era, when people put a lot more focus just on Christmas Day.

Twelfth cake survives in the UK in one place – London's Drury Lane Theatre – where an eighteenth-century actor called Robert Baddeley left a legacy to the theatre to supply a Twelfth cake every year going forward. But it is the only remnant of what was once a night for really riotous fun. Rachel McCormack says that over the Channel it is a very different story. In both France and Spain, Twelfth Night is still celebrated, and is very much a family occasion. In Spain it is the Three Kings Day, and it's the kings who bring your presents – not Santa. They also have a cake, called roscón de reyes, which is a sweet brioche topped with candied fruit – brightly coloured to imitate jewels. There are two tokens hidden in it – a bean, which means you have to pay for the cake, and a figurine, which makes you the king and you get to wear the crown that comes with it.

What can I do with all the dried fruit I invariably buy in a fit of enthusiasm in December and fail to make into mincemeat or cake or, indeed, anything else. Should I just snack on it?

Sophie Wright says dried fruit does make a good snack – indeed, it is one of your five a day – but beware, for it is very high in sugar. So eat in moderation. A cup of grapes is about 60kcal, while a cup of raisins will come out around 500kcal. They're high in fibre, and good for you, but you may regret it if you eat too much.

Sophie advises rehydrating your fruit in alcohol (raisins take to booze particularly well). Then you can either stir it through some ice cream for a quick dessert, or make a semifreddo, which is just whipped cream, whipped egg whites and sugar, all beaten well together. Add in your boozy fruits and just freeze it in a loaf tin.

Tim Anderson agrees. Prunes in port are a classic. From the pages of *The Anderson Family Cookbook* comes a fake Polynesian recipe, popular in Tiki-themed bars in the 1960s, but which became a family favourite for the simple reason that it is delicious. It may remind you of devils on horseback (done with prunes) or oysters on horseback (with oysters). Jay suggested an alternative name for this could simply be 'filth on horseback.'

Tim's Uncle Eric's rumaki

Can be made with chicken livers, water chestnuts, scallops, pineapple or port-soaked prunes. Simply cut whatever you are using into bite-sized pieces, then wrap them with strips of bacon that have been marinated in soy sauce. Secure the strips with a cocktail stick and grill slowly until the bacon is crisp.

Rachel McCormack has two suggestions for you. Firstly, run dried fruit through your stuffing. But also, bring back the dead fly pie. Until the 1980s, it was everywhere, and now, for whatever reason, it's gone. It's just raisins, sultanas, whatever dried fruit you have, sugar, cinnamon, cloves and alcohol if you want to keep it away from any marauding kids. Then you put a layer of shortcrust pastry at the bottom of a buttered tin, put in your fruit mix, another layer of pastry on top, bake it, and that's done. Really easy; time for a revival.

Prof. Barry Smith returns to the snacking conundrum. Pair your dried fruit with whisky, he suggests. Many malts have a lot of dried fruity flavours, and sometimes the right combination of dried fruit and whisky is just the perfect way to while away an evening.

Marmalade

Oranges have been big business at Christmas for a long time. Whether they're sliced and floating on a bowl of steaming punch or are clove-studded and hanging on a tree, we've enjoyed their bright colour and zingy flavours for nearly a thousand years. But while we are all familiar with the sweet or 'China' orange, it's the sharper Seville type that helped to spread Dundee's culinary reputation.

Sue Lawrence says the origins of Keiller's marmalade are well known. The company was founded in 1797. Grocer James Keiller had taken advantage of the opportunity to buy a very cheap consignment of oranges from a ship docking rather late in Dundee harbour. Whether or not he knew they were Seville rather than sweet oranges is moot, but having bought them, he needed to do something with them. The Scots already had quite a reputation for their preserves, and James's wife, Janet, made them into marmalade. From this beginning came a veritable marmalade empire. The Keiller's product was finer cut and less firm in set than most other marmalades around at the time, ideal for selling in jars, rather than cutting into slabs. The beautiful jars became part of the appeal of Dundee marmalade and although Keiller's changed hands and eventually closed in the 1990s, its stone jars remain popular bits of antique-ish paraphernalia.

Besides oranges, what else can I make my marmalade from?

Marmalade is another food around which myth swirls. Like Dundee cake, there's a **persistent rumour it was invented for Mary, Queen of Scots.** But, says Annie Gray, also like Dundee cake, the rumour is rubbish. The clue is in the name: 'marmalade' comes from *marmelo*, Portuguese for 'quince', and from its introduction in the late fifteenth century until the seventeenth century, if you said 'marmalade' to someone, they'd assume you meant quince paste. It was stiff enough to be pressed into blocks and was sometimes stamped with a design. The sugar meant that it was very expensive, and this was a sweetmeat intended for serving after dinner, as part of the banqueting or dessert course. Membrillo paste is really just a Tudor marmalade. So yes, says Annie, you can make marmalade out of anything you want to. It just means (or meant) a very stiff fruit paste. Historic recipe books are full of recipes for apple marmalade, quince marmalade and all sorts of other things. The key is lots of pectin, and an open mind.

Rachel McCormack agrees that quince membrillo-style marmalades are great. She tasted Annie's attempt at Gervase Markham's 1615 Excellent Marmalade of Oranges, which Annie said she was absolutely never making again as she exhibited her burns. Rachel said despite being made with oranges, it was very similar to the quince pastes of Spain, proving that oranges really aren't the only fruit (for marmalade).

If you want to move away from obvious fruits, Rachel says pumpkin is a good alternative. In Mallorca, they make marmalade from Cidra pumpkins. It's a very specific type, and it results in a preserve called cabello de ángel (angel's hair). The pumpkin is grated and then used as you would any other fruit. You can also use courgettes as a serviceable substitute for the Cidras, which are are very hard to get.

Jordan Bourke favours the Korean cousin of marmalade, known as yuja cha in Korean. Yuja (known often in the UK as yuzu, the Japanese name) is a luxury fruit because it takes a long time to grow and for the tree to develop each year to bear good fruit. To make yuja cha, you halve the yuja and thinly slice them, including the skin and pith. Throw away the seeds and put everything, skin and flesh, into a bowl. Add in sugar (about three-quarters sugar to the volume of yuja), and combine everything together. Then pack this into jars, where it will keep almost indefinitely as it's preserved by the sugar. You can use it straight away though: you don't need to wait for weeks. Just add a large spoon into a cup and cover with boiling water and you can drink the tea and eat the yuja. The yuja season is November and December in Korea, and around this time it's drunk a lot. It's a folk remedy, popular for alleviating colds both in Korea and in Japan, where it is so popular that it's sold through vending machines and in convenience stores all winter.

Can the panel inspire me to eat more oranges? I'm particularly keen on something to use up the Sevilles I have left over after making marmalade?

Seville oranges are pippy, pithy and sour. It's not always easy to find uses for them if you've been strict with your recipe and used only what's written. Rob Owen-Brown says you can still enjoy them though. He advises thinking classic and going crêpes Suzette. They are often done with sweet oranges, but there's enough sweetness from the sauce to balance the bitterness. There's no finer way to make oranges sing.

Crêpes Suzette

Segment your oranges, make some pancakes, get a frying pan. Melt some butter in the pan, add some brown sugar and let it start to caramelise with the butter. Throw on some Grand Marnier or triple sec – any orange-flavoured liqueur will work – and end with a splash of double cream and orange juice. You should end up with a butterscotch sauce, which you then just pour over your warmed pancakes, adding the orange segments at the end.

Sophie Wright prefers a savoury dish. She likes a traybake – quick, easy, fuss-free. Just slice some fennel, then take the rind and pith off your oranges, slice them, and put them in a tray. Throw in some fennel seeds, some sliced new potatoes, and then some chicken thighs on top. Brushing each of them with a spoonful of Seville orange marmalade makes them even better. Salt, pepper and bake for about 35 minutes. The legs should be crispy, the potatoes soft, and the oranges will form a lovely mushy sauce, which goes really well with the rest. She normally does it with standard oranges, but as long as you don't mind pips, it would work with Sevilles, in which case add a drizzle of runny honey or maple syrup to balance the bitterness. A splash of orange juice or cider vinegar also helps.

Think of orange as part of a set of balanced flavours, advises Jeremy Pang. Asian cookery is often about finding the balance between bitter, salt, sweet, sour, savoury and spicy. Try a Cantonese pork chop, where you bash out the chop, and then slash it before marinating it. A standard marinade would be something like garlic, light soy sauce, a little bit of sugar, a bit of rice wine, some sesame oil. You're going to deep-fry your chops and serve them with a sauce made from light soy sauce, orange juice (you can use mandarins or other citrus as well), a bit of Worcestershire sauce or tamarind concentrate. Add a bit of marmalade into that and a dash of dark soy – it should give you a perfect balance of sweet and salty.

But Dr Zoe Laughlin has a word of warning. Cooking oranges removes much of their nutritional value. So, if you want to eat more for health reasons, best eat them raw in the bath (or in a G&T, though we'd obviously advise, as ever, drinking responsibly, and do remember you need to eat the slice, not just drink the drink, to get the full benefits).

Top tip: ***The ideal way to carve a turkey***

In Shoreditch we spoke to **Paul Kelly** of Kelly Turkeys, a Guinness World Record holder for turkey plucking and carving. He told us to keep it simple. Remove it from the oven and let it stand, uncovered, to cool enough to cut easily. Don't swaddle it in foil or the skin'll go soggy and it'll continue to (over)cook. Then, once it's rested and isn't going to blister your fingers with scalding steam, take the wing off neatly, then the leg and then the whole breast. You need a very sharp knife, and just follow the keel bone down. Then cut the breast into even slices and cut the meat off the leg. The wing can be cut in half. Note that to beat his world record you'd need to break a 15lb turkey down into 15 equal servings, 180g of white and dark meat, all plated up and given gravy in under 3 minutes and 21 seconds.

Pies

Another of the foods we tend to eat mainly in December are mince pies. Originally made with meat alongside the dried fruit, they're peculiarly British and, as with so many things in life, can be amazing if you've got a good one – and horrible if not. Through many Christmas shows, we've established that they are a very individual taste.

But mince pies really aren't the only pie. It's a topic we love to explore, mainly because we are all a bit obsessed with pastry. If you don't love pie, we'd argue you just haven't met the right one yet (please note, pie is not a euphemism – except in Glasgow, where it really is, much to the embarrassment of most of us, and to the glee of Rachel McCormack). Rob Owen-Brown made a pie to warm the hearts of our Dundee audience, in the shape of Desperate Dan's cow pie. Eight kilos of beef, cow heel (of course) and two horns protruding proudly from the crust.

Besides cow horns, how do I make a really impressive hand-raised pie?

The thought of a proper pie may make us happy, but making one is more of a challenge. Rob says the fear is needless. A basic pork pie is probably the simplest piece of baking you could ever do.

Raised-crust pork pie

You want 575g flour, 200g lard, 220ml water and a good pinch of salt. Water, lard and salt in a pan. Bring it to the boil, then turn the heat straight off. Flour in, beat that until it sort of comes away from the sides of the pan and forms a smooth dough. Then 800g minced fatty pork – so pork shoulder, pork belly – a good pinch of salt, good pinch of pepper. Rob adds puréed onion plus 100g breadcrumbs. Mix that together to form a paste, put it in the fridge, rest. Now get a spring-form tin and grease it well. The next bit is ideal for kids to do because it's like working with meaty playdough. Put a nice thick base of pastry on the bottom of the tin, and then slowly work it up the sides of the tin. Once you've got a little overhang on the edge of the tin, get your pork mix in and then put a lid on it. Fold the sides of the dough over the lid, seal it. An airhole is helpful: just make a hole in the lid, stick in a roll of foil or an icing nozzle or just make a chimney from pastry. Make several if the pie is large. Get it in the oven, 170°C for 2 hours. Pull it out, let it cool for 15 minutes, give everything a good brush with an egg yolk, then back in the oven: 15 minutes on the same temperature. Pull it out, let it cool. Jelly is a winner if you are serving it cold, just make sure you add it when the pie has cooled. Job's done.

That may be impressive enough. But if you are after more, pimp the pork. Try smoked paprika and capers. For an easy build, use pickled eggs to make a gala pie. Want even more? Tim Hayward makes gala pie by using lightly hard-boiled eggs and chopping the ends off, patching them together to make a sort of 'Frankenegg'. But professional butchers use what he calls 'endless egg'. You separate your eggs, knot the end of a chipolata skin and pour in the yolks. Poach that, slip off the skin, slip the egg yolk stick into a bigger skin, and pour in the whites. Poach again, and you've got a three-foot-long egg.

Tim also recommends going wild with the jelly (to those people who don't understand the jelly, the panel doesn't understand you). Make the jelly separately and really think about what it is doing. It isn't there, as it once was, as a preservative: now it is for flavour, texture and to stop the pastry collapsing at the top if your filling has shrunk. So, make it count. Flavour it with port or brandy and, if you have some left over, set it and chop it up to serve with the pie like a sparkly set of jewels.

I like a hefty pie, but pork seems a bit obvious. What are the panel's recommendations for a really interesting pie?

Rachel McCormack says pies are big business in Scotland. Scotch pies are sometimes known as football pies, served, you've guessed it, at football matches (usually accompanied by hot Bovril or similar warming stuff). There's a yearly competition for the best football pie – as well as regular scandals when one proves to be full of the kind of stuff you'd probably prefer not to eat. Traditional Scotch pies are made from well-seasoned mutton, and Sue Lawrence says for her, growing up in Dundee, mutton-filled Scotch pies are deeply nostalgic.

They have a high wall around the top, a good crust, and when you bite into them the mutton grease and juices scald your chin. Not exotic, not spicy, just lovely.

Scotch pies today have branched out. Rachel's seen haggis and tatties, macaroni and cheese, curry – anything imaginable. A pie is really just a container – so anything you'd stew you can put in a pie. And that doesn't just mean meat.

Paula McIntyre brought us a pie with a walnut crust, filled with leeks, triple cream cheese, Parmesan and a home-made curd cheese. Don't neglect, either, the time-honoured combination of potatoes and onions. Cheap and amazingly tasty, it was a working-class staple, and really stands the test of time. In Lancashire, where it's still very popular, it's known as butter pie and it's made with shortcrust pastry, new potatoes and, classically, softened (sweated) onions. And butter, of course, lots of butter. Rob Owen-Brown says he grew up eating them with baked beans or, even better, deep-fried and put in a muffin.

You can also play with your pastry. Try an alternative top – potatoes, pasta, breadcrumbs, turnips all work well. But we'd like to be clear, for it's a question that comes up regularly and we are unanimous on the answer, a casserole dish with a pastry lid – no, it is not a pie. It's a stew with a lid on. And yes, that is our definitive answer.

Top tip: ***How to cook roast potatoes***

Rob Owen-Brown says it's simple. First, use the right potato: a King Edward or a Maris Piper is ideal. Peel them (Rachel McCormack says skin-on roasties are her pet hate). Cut into equal pieces, then three-quarters cook them in boiling water. Shake them off, allow to cool a bit and dry out and then, while they still have a bit of warmth, get them into a pan of red-hot animal fat. Duck, goose, bacon or lard. Roll them around to cover, get them in the oven, turn once and add so much salt you think your doctor will start crying. And pepper, of course.

Other tips? Andi Oliver agrees that animal fat is amazing but says a mixture of olive oil and butter is also surprisingly lovely. Rapeseed works too, says Paula McIntyre, who also rolls hers in a bit of semolina before she gets them in the oil. Meanwhile, Tim Hayward adds that ham hock stock is brilliant for parboiling potatoes. It's too salty to use for much else, but in this case it adds heaps of flavour.

Leftover cookery

We've talked about pies but missed one particular version, which seems to be a seasonal staple with some of you. Sophie Wright's family make it every year and know it as Pepper pie (not named for the spice, but Sophie's married name). It's just all of the various bits left from Christmas dinner – turkey, bacon, gravy, bread sauce, sprouts – the works, chopped roughly, put in a pie, and baked. You can do it as a pastry-covered stew as well, shoving everything into a casserole dish and topping it with puff pastry. Sophie says it's the best pie she knows.

'I don't know what it is with this Christmas leftover obsession! Can't we just set ourselves up better? You've got too much pudding? Buy a smaller pudding! Don't like turkey curry? Buy a smaller turkey!' – Tim Hayward

We are asked about leftovers every January. Annie Gray says it's time we stopped thinking of them as some sort of shabby second. In previous decades, food left over from a previous meal was just seen as ready-cooked ingredients. Plan for them. Integrate them into other meals. It wasn't until the widespread use of fridges in the 1960s that we had the luxury of bunging stuff into cold storage and worrying about what to do with it. Prior to then, you used it quickly, and you used it well. Food was anything up to about a third of the household budget, so if it was food, you ate it.

But what can you do with some of the common suspects? Christmas pudding? Rob Owen-Brown says it's great at the bottom of a Bakewell tart – sweet pastry case, crushed-up Christmas pudding, little bit of brandy on it, frangipane on top. Just get that in the oven and it'll be the best Bakewell you've ever tasted. What about Christmas cake? Sophie Wright says it makes great granola bars – it's largely the same ingredients anyway.

Christmas cake granola bars

Crumble up your Christmas cake, add some macadamia nuts and pecans – or whatever you have in the fridge. Some seeds, oats, honey, lots of butter, and pack it all really tightly into a tray. Bake for about an hour and leave it to set.

Granola bars often crumble when cut, so Sophie's top tip is to freeze the whole tray, and then cut them up and allow them to defrost. That way they will hold their shape.

Jordan Bourke has another way to use Christmas cake. Crumble it up and put it into a bottle of vodka. It looks appalling, but all that spice and dried fruit sweetness mingles really well with the alcohol. Add some lemon and orange zest and maybe a cinnamon stick and you can just drink it neat or mixed with lemonade, whatever you fancy. Zoe Laughlin tasted it and said it was 'dangerously good.'

I always do a gammon over Christmas, just in case. But just in case doesn't always happen, and I need some quick fixes to use it fast when I finally decide no-one is going to come and help me out.

Tim Hayward remarks that the key here is to remember what gammon is. It's the best bit of the pig, usually the back leg, which has been brined or dry-cured, and often smoked. It's basically posh bacon. And yes, you've already boiled (or baked) it, but that shouldn't stop you thinking of it as bacon. Sliced thinly, fried in plenty of fat, it'll be the best bacon sandwich you've ever tasted. Zoe Laughlin agrees, but also disagrees. She prefers to slice it thickly, grilling it and serving it with hot buttered toast, mustard and ketchup.

A sandwich is a really good solution, says Jordan Bourke, but come on, it's Christmas. Use your imagination. Lots of people eat Christmas cake with cheese, especially in the North, so build on that. He likes a gammon and cheese sandwich with crumbled Christmas cake in it – it works like chutney, giving you a suitably seasonal twist.

Sophie Wright says you can do anything you would with bacon – don't limit yourself to simple sandwiches. How about a risotto? Start with a basic risotto mix, so sweated off onions and garlic, risotto rice, white wine and stock. Add your gammon halfway through cooking, so that the salt in it can start to season the risotto. Then, at the end, add a really big handful of peas and some chopped fresh mint, lemon zest and Parmesan. It'll be delicious.

That's not all. If you plan ahead and cook enough, you'll also have leftover risotto, and that makes arancini. And if you've got leftover arancini, they can be squashed flat and put in a sandwich and then you can deep-fry the sandwich and … we'll stop there. But leftovers are great.

Top tip: ***How to deshell a hard-boiled egg***

We had a lot of discussion on this but had to bow to the wisdom of one plucky audience member in Rochester (subsequent trials have proven their point). It's remarkably easy once you know the knack, which is to use a teaspoon. It slides up between egg white and shell splendidly, easing the shell off without the need for holding it under running water, long fingernails, or any of the other tricks you might have heard. Crack the base of the egg where the air hole is and remove just enough shell to insert your spoon. Then go from there.

Is a garlic press naughty or nice?

When we ran a Twitter poll on the subject of garlic presses, over 8000 of you responded: 56.7% of you said it was incredible, the rest of you were less convinced. Our panel was equally divided.

Jordan Bourke: Very much a garlic press defender. 'They've been much maligned and I'm fed up with it.' It is a vital tool when you need to crush garlic quickly, and as for all the nonsense people spout about being able to tell the difference in texture in a dish – just no.

Annie Gray: Has room for hers, which is a single piece of slightly curved metal with large holes at the downward sweep of the curve. You rock it over a peeled clove, and then thwack it on a board to release any extra bits.

Sue Lawrence: Not a convert. 'Mine have always been the hinged type, which I hate as they are so impossible to clean.'

Jeremy Pang: Just use a cleaver.

Rob Owen-Brown: Best thing to do with one is to fish it out of the dishwasher, stare hard at the bits caught in it, and drop it in the bin.

And finally, we asked our audience in Dundee about incidents involving mistaken ingredients.

One audience member has a lesson for the language learners among you. She once explained to French friends of hers that she tried to avoid foods with too many condoms in them. *Préservatifs* ... not to be confused with *agents de conservateurs alimentaires*, unless you, too, want to experience the French stare of stupefaction.

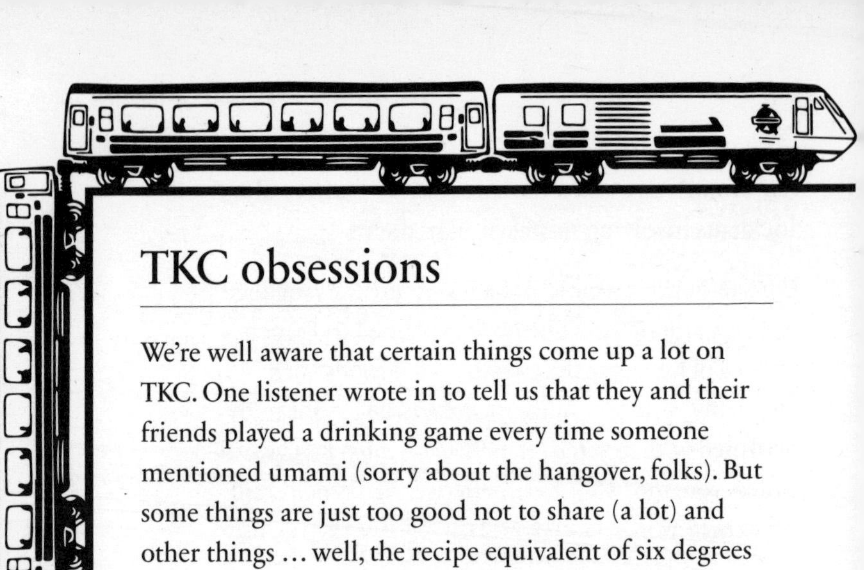

TKC obsessions

We're well aware that certain things come up a lot on TKC. One listener wrote in to tell us that they and their friends played a drinking game every time someone mentioned umami (sorry about the hangover, folks). But some things are just too good not to share (a lot) and other things ... well, the recipe equivalent of six degrees of separation might just be to see how long it takes before someone suggests adding bacon or deep-frying it. To see how much attention you've been paying over the 336 pages/nearly 10 years:

How many times have we mentioned the following in the course of this book? Bonus points if you can also match the panellist/s most often responsible for them:

a) Umami (bonus points if it is synergistic)
b) The Barbara Cartland cookbook
c) The Manchester egg
d) The Almost-Patented Baked Potato Method
e) Candle salad
f) Mythbuster klaxon
g) Add bacon
h) Deep-fry it
i) Aphrodisiacs
j) *The Anderson Family Cookbook*

Answers, in the time-honoured fashion, are at the bottom of the page.

Answers: a) 22 (Barry Smith); b) 2 (Rachel McCormack); c) 3 (Rob Owen-Brown); d) 2 (Zoe Laughlin); e) 3 (Annie Gray); f) 10 (Annie Gray); g) 48 (everyone); h) 10 (everyone); i) 6 (Jay Rayner); j) 3 (Tim Anderson)

Index

Acknowledgements

This book is the brainchild of the TKC production company, Somethin' Else. They've championed the show and the book from the start, so a huge hoorah to them for everything related to it.

Specific thanks to: Darby Dorras for basically being the All Seeing Eye; Hannah Newton for her microscopic knowledge of the show for ever; my crack transcription team: Jemima Rathbone, Millie Chu and Caragh Burstow Green for sorting out who said what and how 'pink, grapefruit and your genitalia' isn't actually a cocktail (on a related note, I would like to proffer undying irritation at whoever made the transcription software that can't cope with accents, long words or, in fact, people). I still don't know what 'a sticky sort of wreck cupboard, young anxious mess is' (and it'll probably ruin it if I find out). Heartfelt thanks to Mohit Bakaya, Denis Nowlan and Daniel Clarke at Radio 4 for originally commissioning the show, supporting the book, and continuing to transmit our frequently innuendo-ridden conversations to the nation on Saturday mornings.

Huge thanks to Jay, of course, for keeping us all in line while encouraging us to be ourselves, for his secret talent as 'The Train Whisperer', and for providing the foreword to end all forewords. Thanks to all of my fellow panellists, past and present. Writing this has made me realise even more than before how bloody brilliant you all are.

My agent, Tim Bates, has been his usual suave and supportive self (we met through TKC so I guess this is a bit of a love-in really).

At Ebury, Kay Halsey and Nell Warner have edited and overseen the process of making a fast-paced panel show into a quirky almanac. Thanks also to Jonathan Baker and David Wardle for designing and illustrating our innermost thoughts. Meanwhile, Esther Wilson has proved a researcher extraordinaire, furkling out all sorts of foodie facts.

Thanks also to the usual band of friends and family, who didn't actually know I was writing this for most of the time, but were nevertheless there all the way through. The Gin & Crisps gang, Hare & Tortoises (yes, I wrote this during lockdown, I love a good WhatsApp group), Laura, Bex & C, Kathy (and Bess), thank you all. Finally, to Matt, sorry about the shrieks of laughter and occasional loud swearing on your Zoom calls but see above re transcription software.

Finally, to our audience. We'd be nothing without you. Thank you for listening, thank you for your questions, and here's to another decade of *The Kitchen Cabinet*.

Production credits

The Kitchen Cabinet is a Somethin' Else Production for BBC Radio 4. Darby Dorras is the Executive Producer, Hannah Newton is the Senior Producer, Laurence Bassett, Dan Cocker and Jemima Rathbone are the Producers, and are supported by Assistant Producers Rosie Merotra and Millie Chu. Additional production is from Steve Ackerman.

Outside Broadcast engineering is by Paul Nickson and Paul Brogden, and the mix engineers are Josh Gibbs and Gulliver Tickell.

Thanks go to the countless many others for their help on production over the years too.

1

BBC Books, an imprint of Ebury Publishing
20 Vauxhall Bridge Road,
London SW1V 2SA

BBC Books is part of the Penguin Random House group of companies whose addresses can be found at global.penguinrandomhouse.com

Main text by Annie Gray
Foreword by Jay Rayner

This book is published to accompany the BBC Radio 4 broadcast *The Kitchen Cabinet*, produced by Somethin' Else.

First published by BBC Books in 2021

www.penguin.co.uk

A CIP catalogue record for this book is available from the British Library

ISBN 9781785947162

Designed and set by seagulls.net
Illustrations by David Wardle

Printed and bound in Great Britain by Clays Ltd, Elcograf S.p.A

Penguin Random House is committed to a sustainable future for our business, our readers and our planet. This book is made from Forest Stewardship Council® certified paper.